Handbook of Dog Care

P9-BHS-945

Contents

	Page
Journal of Our Dog	Inside Cover
The Dog in the Family	2
The Story of the Dog	4
So You're Getting a Dog	8
Purebred or Mixed Breed?	12
Your First Day with Your Dog	16
How to Feed Your Dog	19
How to Housebreak Your Puppy	25
Your Dog's Health	29
Grooming Your Dog	39
Puppies on the Way	43
Spaying and Neutering—The Facts of Life	47
The Dog Owner's Responsibilities	49
How to Travel with Your Dog	52
How to Correct Bad Habits	54
Simple Obedience Training	60
Some Tricks To Teach Your Dog	68
Dog Breeds of the World	74
Dog Breeds and Registration	92
How to Understand a Dog Show	95
Training Your Dog for a Dog Show	99
Opportunities in the World of Dogs	103

A Publication of THE PURINA DOG CARE CENTER
Checkerboard Square • St. Louis, Missouri 63188
Copyright 1979, Ralston Purina Co.

The Dog in the Family

A traditional picture of happiness is one in which the family is gathered about the fireplace at night while winter winds blow snow and cold outside. There will be a family dog in that picture, too, lying at length on the warm floor, his back so close to the fire you cannot imagine why he doesn't singe his fur.

This picture conveys to us a sense of shelter and warmth, of protection, and of being well fed. And perhaps it stirs us so because we can almost cast our memories back to a time 15,000 years ago when primitive hunters crouched between a cliff and a fire, striving to protect themselves from the cold, and from wild beasts that waited in the darkness beyond the fire.

The dog belongs in that picture, too. For in that time so long ago, the dog cast his lot with man. Dog and man have moved together down the centuries, changing and adapting themselves as the times required, until today when dogs are just as common in apartment houses as they are in the country.

Men have taken their dogs with them wherever they went. And the dogs, showing both marvelous intelligence and remarkable adaptability, have worked to help man, to earn their own share in the partnership. In the Arctic they have been sled dogs. They have chased game in the deserts and across mountain ranges. The Ainus of Japan have taught them to swim out into shallow ocean bays and to herd schools of fish to the beaches. Dogs have pulled burdens tied to two poles, called "travois" by the Plains Indians.

They have served as scout, messenger, and Red Cross dogs. They have fought by the side of soldiers in ancient armies as well as in our modern armies. So far back as we can trace man's history, the dog has been the guardian of his flocks. He has protected them from wolves and hyenas, has located the lost and returned them to the flock, and has learned how to drive them to pasture, to the fold, or to the market.

Beyond all these things, the dog has been a companion to man, even serving as eyes for the blind and ears for the deaf. For that reason, both are happier when the dog is in the home. Not so long ago, the dog lived in the barn, or under it. He scavenged for food, and was given the leftovers.

Today the dog has his honored place in the home. He helps get the kids off to school in the morning, naps while they study, barks at strangers, romps with the children when they come home, takes the warmest spot by the fireside, or sleeps on the warm-air register.

And for that, he'll get more pampering and loving than all the rest of the family put together. Why not? He's the family dog—our dog!

The Story of the Dog

If you look at a dog and then at a wolf, coyote, or fox, you will see that they are similar in many respects. But if you compare a dog to a cat or to a grizzly bear, you will think them very different animals indeed. Yet some 40 million years ago there were no wolves, dogs, cats, or bears, no foxes or coyotes, but only the common ancestor of them all.

Scientists call this long-extinct animal *Miacis* (pronounced My-a-Kiss). He wasn't very big. But then horses were only lamb-sized, and many of the other animals we know today either did not exist or are represented by animals which weren't very big either.

If you visit a zoo or look in a library book on mammals, you can see the civet, or civet cat. *Miacis* looked something like the civet. He had a long body, even longer tail, and short legs. He probably was a forest dweller and might have lived in trees. He probably had retractile claws like cats.

As geologic ages passed, some of the descendants of *Miacis* evolved gradually into bears. They became heel-walkers. Some of them became giants. Cats became solitary hunters and began to depend upon their claws to capture food.

While deer, horses, cattle, and other grazing animals were developing the ability to live on the great grasslands, some of *Miacis'* descendants became running animals in order to capture their food. From these ancient running animals has come the dog family, both wild and domestic. They are called *Canidae*, or *canids*. From that family name comes our word *canine*.

Now if you ask what a dog is, the answer must be in two parts. The dog is a physical being, made thus and so. He is also a mental creature which, because of his structure and his past, acts thus and so.

4

First of all, the dog is a mammal. A mammal gives birth to live young, nurses its young by mammary or milk-producing glands, and is more or less covered with hair. Man himself is a mammal, so we have to find a more specific definition for the dog.

The dog is a four-footed animal designed for the chase. He runs on his toes, whereas his distant relative, the bear, walks on his heels. His claws do not retract as do those of his long-ago cousin, the cat.

His jaws are designed for grasping, and the teeth for cutting and tearing. He grows two sets of teeth. The first set, the "milk" teeth, fall out at about four months, to be replaced by 42 permanent ones.

The dog hasn't any starch-breaking enzymes in his saliva, and no masticating and grinding teeth as humans have. So it is "proper" for him to gulp or bolt his food.

Most dogs are said to have "nose brains." This is because he depends chiefly upon his nose to bring him knowledge of the world about him. He can, for instance, smell one part of urine in 60 million parts of water. This is important to remember, and will be useful to you in housebreaking your dog.

Dogs, both wild and domestic, smell prominent objects, such as lampposts, fireplugs, automobile tires, and stumps to check "territorial boundaries."

By smelling these "signposts," the dogs know what other dogs are in the neighborhood, their sex and whether they are friends or enemies. And because of odors brought by the feet of other dogs, they may know where they had been.

But the dog is also a dog because of "sociability." The pariah dogs of Egypt live in highly organized societies. Wolves live in packs and obey pack laws, which include helping each other. Contrast this with the solitary lives of cats, or the aloof family life of foxes.

If you watch dogs closely, you'll sometimes see signs of this pack sociability.

Domestication Of The Dog

But the dog is also a domestic animal. This means two things. He is tame and is willing to obey man's laws, and he has cast in his lot with man. No one knows how or why the domestication of any animal took place, nor even when. But the dog was probably the first domestic animal, and he probably became fully domestic 15 to 20 thousand years ago. Almost complete skeletons, dating back to 7000 B.C. have been found.

Here is one of the many theories about how the dog became domesticated.

Primitive hunters brought wolf puppies home and tamed them. A species of wolves with an inferiority complex developed. Unable to compete with wolves, they haunted man's campfires, and lived on his garbage. Being animals of the chase, and being used to cooperating in it, they joined the ancient hunters in the excitement of the chase. Men recognized the value of these animals, and so gradually a partnership was formed.

Whatever theory is advanced, you must not forget that the major decision had to come from the dogs themselves. Dogs closely resemble wolves, though no scientist today will say that dogs have developed from any living wolf family. But the wolf is a wild animal. So are all but one species of cat. So are bears. Thus it is evident that the dogs *wanted to* join man.

What is perhaps more important to you is that the men of prehistory were great animal breeders. They knew and understood animals. They had to understand them in order to live with them and survive. Prehistoric men left a fabulous legacy, for they developed races of dogs with different aptitudes and instincts.

Have you ever wondered why some dogs chase cars? Why some fight silently, others with great snarling? Why some slash and tear, while others grab and hang on? Why some dogs test the wind for scent, while others trail? Why dogs can be house-broken but monkeys or horses cannot?

As individual dogs began to show certain inborn aptitudes, primitive men developed these into races of dogs, according to their needs. A shepherd dog, for instance, had to have a sense of property-owning or guarding. He had to drive cattle or sheep by nipping at their heels, for to tear and slash would have crippled or stampeded them. He had to fight silently, since a great noise might stampede the herd.

But the coursing dog, trying to run down game, had to slash with his teeth. For the game might be too big for him to bring down until it had been badly crippled. And, when brought to bay, it might also kill him unless the dog could dash in, slash, and then jump away.

The monkey is highly intelligent. But he can't be house-broken. Nor can the horse, cow, or canary. But dogs and cats can be. It is probably because they inherit from ancient Miacis the den dweller's instinct to keep his bed and home clean.

You can watch this instinct working in any litter of puppies. As soon as they are able to walk, they wobble away from the nest to relieve themselves.

So You're Getting a Dog

It is very cruel to animals not to prepare in advance for the arrival of a dog. You have many things to think about first. For example, are you going to keep your dog in the house or are you going to make him stay in the back yard, a farm building, or garage?

Your first consideration is what breed to get. Dogs are very adaptable and learn to fit into most situations. But there are some points you must consider.

What size dog do you want? Most big dogs need ample room. The largest breeds like the Great Dane and St. Bernard, often get along very well in small areas. They are so big they do not romp about as much as some smaller dogs.

The intermediate-size dogs—German Shepherds, Boxers, Doberman Pinschers, and others—are built for heavy work. They have a vast store of energy and need exercise while growing. Once grown, they fit into small homes quite well.

The toys and terriers are great home dogs. They are the right size for almost any home but they may have disadvantages, too. For example, if you want a hunting dog you'd hardly settle for a Chihuahua.

It should be said here that all dogs do better if they are allowed to live and grow up in the house. They learn better manners, they are happier, and they learn faster than do dogs kept tied in the yard. So, even if you want to get a hunting dog, you may plan to keep him in the house.

If, however, you do have to keep the dog outside, then you must consider the problems of a dog pen and doghouse before you get your dog. Many people make the mistake of building pens that are too large. Since dogs, except puppies, seldom exercise for its own sake, they will not use the space in big pens, but will only make it harder and more expensive to keep up.

A kennel run 10 feet wide and 20 feet long is bigger than average and will serve for most dogs. The best fencing is steel, galvanized and woven into what often is called "storm fencing." Most kennel fencing should be six feet high, since it usually will prevent the dog from climbing over it. Cattle fencing is not often satisfactory. The heaviest grade of chicken wire will do, however, if it is inch mesh or less.

A dog will live in a mudhole unless some surface is put into the run. Probably the best material is a medium size round gravel. Paved runs are very expensive and are considered hard on a dog's feet. But they have many advantages. They are easily disinfected and can be laid so as to permit good drainage.

Outdoor kennels are best if they have two compartments. In such a kennel, the dog goes in, turns into the end of the box, and jumps into the second compartment. This keeps the direct wind from him. It is most important to keep your dog out of the draft, whatever the method of construction. If the roof is on hinges, cleaning is easy. Wine barrels also make excellent dog kennels.

Dog house building plans can be obtained from a number of sources. But the main points are these:

■ *The kennel should be off the ground sufficiently to prevent water from leaking in.*
■ *It should not be too big, else the dog will be unable to heat it in the winter.*
■ *It should have an overhang at the door to prevent rain from beating in. The roof should slope.*

Sometimes it will be too expensive to have a fenced pen. In such cases, and for house dogs as well, you can put up a wire run. This is done by stringing a heavy wire from, say, the back porch to a tree in the yard. A thick ring or roller is put on the wire and a leash is fastened to this. One end of the leash, or another leash, is fastened to the dog's collar. When these are all hooked together, the dog can run from one end of the wire to the other. He can be taught to relieve himself at one end of the run. Similarly a heavy wire or cable may be on the ground stretched between 2 posts. Pets should not be on outside metal leads attached to trees during lightning storms.

House dogs should be taken on escorted walks, which they will enjoy most. You should plan in advance to work out a regular schedule of walks and to have regular play hours with your puppy. After dogs are grown, escorted evening walks will do and dogs can be taught to use the wire run for other purposes.

As pointed out, the exercise requirements of dogs vary greatly. So do their requirements in being taken out for relief. These requirements will depend upon how many times a day you feed, how much feed you offer, and how much water the dog drinks.

Before getting a dog, there are some things you must find out about the dog himself. You should learn whether he has been wormed; how long ago it was; whether worms were found; and what kind they were.

Next, you'll want to know whether the dog has had any protection from distemper or hepatitis. This will depend somewhat on the dog's age. The breeder may feel that his puppies will enjoy an immunity given in their mother's milk. So if the pups haven't been weaned they may not have had shots. Even if the pup you are getting is 10 to 12 weeks old and has had serum protection, you should consult your veterinarian immediately about active protection.

Finally, you'll want to know about registration papers. If your puppy is purebred, the breeder should be able to give you a four-generation copy of the puppy's pedigree and an application form to register a puppy from a registered litter. Some breeders register puppies at the time they register the litter. In such cases, he merely signs over the dog's registration to you. You should have the papers transferred so that ownership of the dog is in your name.

It is important that you get the papers at the time you get your puppy. If you don't, you might never get them. If the papers aren't available when you get your puppy, obtain a written statement from the breeder that you will get your papers within a certain time, or your money back.

At the time you purchase your puppy, registration papers may not appear important to you. But the time may come when you'll want to show your dog because it has turned out to have a superior rating. Or you may wish to compete in obedience trials. If your dog is a female, the day may come when you'll want her to have pups. If your dog is a male, owners of females may want to breed to him. So, if papers are available, get them.

Summary

Make adequate preparations for your dog before you get him. These include family discussions as to the type and whether he'll live in the house or out of doors.

Decide what kind of outdoor quarters you will use. Don't make your kennel pen too large. Make the kennel itself wind- and rain-proof. Find out from the breeder what protection your dog has been given by vaccination, and whether he has been wormed. Insist on a written contract about registration papers if they are not available at the time of purchase. Make arrangements to have your new puppy or dog examined by a veterinarian to determine the dog's state of health and the veterinarian's recommendations regarding vaccinations.

Purebred or Mixed Breed?

What breed is your dog? Is it purebred? Or is it a member of that large family of dogs who are considered mixed breeds?

Every dog whose ancestry is unknown is a member of this "mixed breed" family. These dogs sometimes are called mongrels, and each one usually will have characteristics all his own.

Purebred dogs conform to type, because of the fashion of breeders, or they have aptitudes for certain kinds of work which have been cultivated in them. Yet they are still dogs. The purebreds cannot be more than dogs and the mongrels cannot be less.

Your dog, purebred or "mixed," is a direct descendant of those first domesticated dogs of prehistory. And he may even be a descendant of some of the famous dogs of history. As you watch your dog and work with him and come to know him better, you may be able to visualize how his characteristics could have made his ancestors "dogs of history." And you may want to sit with your dog beneath a shady oak some morning and dream or talk with him about his family tree and how his distant relatives got to America.

The Indians of North and South America had dogs at the time of Columbus. The Spanish Conquistadores saw dozens of animals which they called dogs because they had no words of their own for them.

Dogs may have come from Asia by the early land bridge between Siberia and Alaska. Dogs were in America as early as 4000 B.C.

Columbus had what he called a Greyhound on his first voyage; on his second, a dog he called a Mastiff. He also had war dogs trained in Spain. The most famous of these Mastiffs were Becerillo and his son, Leoncido. Leoncido belonged to Balboa, the discoverer of the Pacific Ocean, and was one of the smartest and most ferocious dogs in history.

Leoncido taught the Spaniards many lessons, even to have mercy. Thus, Balboa was taking his siesta one day when an aged women came to his armed camp seeking help for her people. The soldiers thought they would enjoy watching Leoncido attack her. But the dog sniffed her and then ignored her. Balboa, awakened, ruled that he could not show less mercy than his dog.

John and Sebastian Cabot brought dogs to Nova Scotia and Canada. There was at least one dog on the Mayflower, and the English appear to have brought dogs to North America even before the Mayflower came.

So you are entitled to dream that your dog is a descendant of those dogs that came with the discoverers and colonizers. And you'll be more than half right, too.

If you have a mixed breed and you want to try to guess his ancestry, you can work on the problem from two ways. One is by studying his conformation. You can say: "He looks like ...". And the second way is by observing his actions. You can conclude that "He acts like ...". You'll probably never know the truth, but you can have some fun, and you'll understand dogs better while doing it.

Scientists often catalog dogs by their jaw lengths. There are long-jawed breeds such as the Doberman Pinscher, German Shepherd, Greyhound, English and Irish Setters, and others. And there are short-muzzled dogs, such as the St. Bernard, Chow Chow, Chihuahua, Pomeranian, and others.

With some of these breeds, such as the Doberman Pinscher and the German Shepherd, there is a tendency, which is inherited, to be minus some of their premolars. Thus, the jaw length, plus the absence of teeth, might give you a clue.

Please do not confuse the short nose or short jaw with the pushed-in face of such breeds as Pekingese, Bulldogs, and Boston Terriers. These are difficult features to keep, even in purebreds. In mixed breeds the pushed-in face seldom is seen, though it may be slightly discernible in crossbreds.

The ears also may be a clue. Spaniels and Poodles have longer than normal ears. So do Bassets and Bloodhounds. It is not known for certain, but it is believed that all prehistoric dogs had erect ears such as wolves, jackals, foxes, and hyenas have. So erect ears might indicate shepherd dog ancestry of some kind, or Arctic sled dog, or Chow blood. Drooping ears could indicate Spaniel, Poodle, or Hound ancestry.

Some dogs, with very fine, short coats, become nearly hairless. This does not indicate Mexican or Chinese Hairless ancestry. More likely it is a sign of disease called alopecia, or falling hair. But hair type can give you a clue.

Long, standoffish guard hair is a characteristic of the Chow Chow, and of many Arctic dogs. Long bristles that lie flat indicate some of the shepherd types. Hair which has a tendency not to fall out, but to get frizzy and curly, could indicate some terrier blood.

Very short, fine hair is a characteristic of Dachshunds, Whippets, Miniature Pinschers, and similar dogs. The presence of a strong spotting pattern would indicate Dalmatian ancestry.

That ancient first ancestor of the dog, *Miacis,* had a long back. Dog people have been trying to breed out this tendency in most breeds for a very long time.

But German Shepherds are longer in body than they are tall. So are Dachshunds, Welsh Corgis, and a few others. A long-backed, short-legged, drop-eared dog would indicate Dachshund blood. If he had the first two characteristics, but erect ears, he might easily have some Corgi blood in him.

And now consider the possible ancestry of your dog just by studying his actions.

Dogs that chase cars, bicycles, and running children inherit strong herding or cattle-driving instincts. The cattle-driving instinct is especially strong if the dog nips at the heels, without really trying to bite.

Some dogs grab and shake when trying to kill some creature or while fighting. This is a strong terrier instinct — the centuries-old methods of the great ratter. Dogs inheriting Greyound instincts slash with their teeth, and duck in and out like great prize fighters. They also love to get out and run, whether or not they are chasing something.

In fighting, some dogs grab, then begin to chew while holding on, trying to get more of the enemy into their jaws. This is a habit developed in the Bulldogs and other pit-fighting dogs of the past. So if your dog shows such tendencies, he might have Bull Terrier or Bulldog blood in him.

If, while out in the field, your dog tests wind scents instead of trailing foot scents (tracking), then he might have Setter, Pointer, or Spaniel blood in him. If he tracks, then he should have some hound ancestry. If he's crazy about jumping into cold water and just swimming about, he probably has Spaniel, Poodle or Retriever ancestry.

All these clues can make owning a mixed breed a lot of fun. You might even make a catalog of all the traits your dog shows. And in that case, you'd really find that your dog is ALL dog.

Summary

Purebred dogs are bred to transmit specific characteristics. But you should remember that all dogs—"mixed" or purebred —share a common ancestry. They are all dog. Many of the "mixed breeds" of America are descendants of dogs brought here by the original explorers, and by the Mayflower. Try to guess the ancestry of your dog by his conformation and by studying the ways in which he does things.

Your First Day with Your Dog

When you are getting a new puppy, it is important that you get him in the morning. It is preferable that this be on a Saturday morning, so that you will have a long weekend in which to get acquainted with your dog. By getting him in the morning, the dog will have a long day in which to get acquainted with you.

If you have a long distance to drive for the puppy, ask the breeder not to feed him in the morning, since your puppy might become carsick during the trip home. Give your puppy his first Purina puppy foods in your home when he is very hungry so he will know he can depend on you.

On the trip home, hold the puppy on your lap and give him as much opportunity as possible to get your particular odor. Remember, dogs have "nose brains" and you want your puppy's nose to tell him as soon as possible that you are his master. Take along a large bath towel just in case puppy gets sick.

In the chapter on Housebreaking, you are told how to build a box bed for your puppy. Presumably you have prepared for his arrival by building the box in advance. You should put some of your old clothes in this box so that puppy will continue to get your smell and be comforted and assured by it.

During this first day, puppy should be taken out every hour. Take him to a preselected spot, as pointed out in the chapter on Housebreaking. Remember that you must take him out before play, after eating, when he awakens from a nap, and before anything exciting is likely to happen.

Where puppy has had an accident, wash the area with soap and water, then use a nicotine sulphate or ammonia solution on the spot, as directed in the chapter on Housebreaking.

Practically all people want to play with a new puppy. He'll want to play, too. But puppies tire quickly and want to rest and sleep. So do not allow family members to maul him until he is entirely worn out. Put him in his box bed for his naps.

If, during play, puppy gets too rough, slap him upwards gently under the chin and scold him. Remember, this is the age at which he must be taught he cannot growl or bite.

In handling your puppy, do not pick him up by the front legs. Instead, pick him up by placing a hand under his abdomen. Lift him into your arms and cradle him so that his body lies along your arm.

The breeder may have given you a complicated formula for feeding the puppy. This may involve five feedings a day. Even with some breeds, such as the St. Bernard, where the growth curve is extremely rapid, this is not necessary if you keep food available at all times. It is wise to use the same diet as the breeder fed for a day or two, then gradually accustom your puppy to the feeding program you've selected. (See Chapter on Feeding.)

If you received registration papers for your puppy when you bought it—as you should—do not file them away somewhere. Instead, send them directly to the registering body. In that way, they won't be mislaid, and you won't put it *off* for years on end. Thousands of people "always meant" to get their dogs registered but delayed until they lost the papers.

Do not give your puppy any water during the evening. Take him out at your own bedtime for his final opportunity to relieve himself. And this is the time to form the habit:

Don't *put* him out, *take* him out. Then you'll always be sure.

When you put him to bed, he'll be lonely and will start to cry. Some of your worn clothes in the bed will help. So will a loud-ticking alarm clock, and perhaps even a toy with which he's become familiar.

He may continue to howl. Soon he'll cry himself to sleep. Sometimes it is necessary to be firm and give puppy a light spanking. But do this as a last resort.

Don't give in and let the puppy out of the box. If you give in once, you are on the road to ruin—and so is your pup. The same thing applies when he awakens at 4 a.m. Don't give in. He has to learn to control his bladder and bowels as well as his loneliness. If you give in once, the job gets harder—and finally impossible.

Summary

Get your dog in the morning. Get him when you have a long weekend ahead. Don't wear him out with too much play. Show him his toilet spot as soon as possible. Don't give in to his crying the first night or two. He'll get accustomed to his box and will regard it as home. Register your dog the day you get the papers. It is best to purchase a 6-8 week old puppy since he'll adjust most readily to a new environment at this time.

How to Feed Your Dog

It is very easy to feed your dog in modern America, although many people make it inexcusably difficult and complicated. The increasing use of commercial dog foods has brought better health and longer life to dogs since these diets contain the proper level and balance of amino acids, fats, carbohydrates, vitamins, minerals and other nutrients for proper nutrition.

There are two types of dog food. One is the home formula, which may consist of anything from table leftovers to breakfast cereals mixed with ground round steak, vegetables, liver, and vitamin supplements. Most of these home formulas are much more expensive than the best brands of commercially prepared foods, and take longer to prepare. But even more important, most do not provide a balanced diet.

The second type is the commercially prepared dog food. It, in turn, can be divided into three general types. One is the dry food, another is the soft-moist and third is canned food. Some foods, such as horse meat, either frozen or canned, are not really a complete dog food, but simply a supplement.

Literally millions of otherwise well-informed people are under the impression that the dry foods are cereals and that canned foods are meat. The fact is that both contain meat proteins, but in the dry foods the water has been removed. A brief description of both types follows:

Dry Dog Foods. Most contain between 21 and 23 percent protein, 8 percent fat, 35 to 45 percent carbohydrates (may be expressed as nitrogen-free extract, or N.F.E., if on the label) and about 10 percent water. This type will deliver from 1300 to 1700 digestible calories per pound.

The dry foods come in several forms. Some of the bulky types are designed to keep dogs from overeating. Some are fed dry, others with water mixed in, and others can be fed either way.

Canned Dog Food. Contains about 9 to 12 percent protein, 6 percent fat, 3 to 5 percent carbohydrates, and up to 78 percent water. The better canned foods will deliver approximately 650 to 700 Calories per pound.

Semi-Moist Dog Food. Contains about 20 percent protein, 7 percent fat, 35 percent carbohydrates and up to 34 percent water. Good quality semi-moist foods contain approximately 1200 digestible Calories per pound.

The better brands of dry, moist and canned dog foods are kept under continuous test at research kennels, where they constantly are checked for nutritional quality.

Feeding Rules
How much you feed will depend upon both you and the dog. Dogs are individuals. If you have two litter mates weighing exactly the same when adult, their nutritional requirements may still differ. It may take more food to maintain the one than the other.

A good rule in feeding mature dogs is: Feed 1 cup of dry food per 10 pounds of body weight per day. Thus, a 30-pound dog with normal activity would get 3 cups of food per day.

When you feed a canned food, remember that it contains about 78 percent water. Therefore, feed one to one and one-half ounces of canned food per pound of dog per day.

This brings us to another rule. If you feed a dry dog food that has been moistened, you may keep food before your puppy at all times but feed your adult only the amount that will be cleaned up in 30 minutes.

When To Feed
The grown dog does very well on one meal a day. Any excess

food can turn into fat or be wasted. Because we eat three meals a day, you may think it cruel to feed your dog only once a day. Yet that is normally adequate for adult dogs unless they are working hard or nursing young.

Do not feed table scraps. You may give the dog more than he should have. He'll get finicky-and maybe even too fat. Between-meal snacks also tend to destroy appetite. Feeding snacks from the table simply makes beggars and nuisances out of dogs.

The best commercial foods, dry, moist or canned, contain more than adequate amounts of vitamins and minerals for normal growth, maintenance and reproduction.

Most people feed their dogs in the evening before their own meal. This helps to keep the dog from begging. But many kennels, and many people having housebreaking troubles, feed in the morning. Still others feed at noon. Morning feeding often is a nuisance to people who are rushing off to school or to work. So, when you feed will be a matter of your own convenience or housebreaking troubles, if you have them.

Feeding the Pregnant Dog
Females carrying puppies require only a small increase in food consumption until the last 20 days of pregnancy when food intake will increase approximately 25%. It is the nutrient quality of the ration that is of utmost importance during this period. Although a lot of nutrients are being stored in the developing pups, the female becomes less active and uses her food more efficiently. For this reason, her food consumption is increased only slightly until the last trimester of pregnancy. Even during this time the female needs only a nutritionally complete dog food and water.

After giving birth to the litter, increased consumption of food takes place to enable quantities of milk to be produced. When the maximum quantity of milk is being produced (about the fourth week), the female is consuming about 2 to 3 times the normal quantity of food.

Weaning
Most pups start eating the same solid foods as their mother about 3 weeks of age and by 5-6 weeks the female has usually started to wean the pups. It is generally recommended that pups be weaned at six weeks and remain on solid food.

At weaning time, the female should not be fed on the day weaning takes place. Feed 1/5 normal maintenance ration the second day, 2/5 the third day, etc., until she is back on normal ration. This helps reduce the quantity of milk the female produces after weaning and helps restore her milk-producing organs to normal.

Feeding Puppies

While the puppies are nursing, they should be watched periodically to be sure all of them get a chance to nurse. As the pups grow, make the ration fed to the mother available to the pups. By the time they are ready to be weaned at six weeks they are already consuming enough food that no setback occurs. You will want to keep Purina puppy foods available to the pups at all times until the pup is 16-20 weeks of age. Thereafter, two feedings a day are sufficient or if the pup doesn't overeat, self-feeding can be continued. Take care that your puppy does not become overweight. Some dogs never recover from being overly fat as a pup and excessive weight is also generally unhealthy.

As a pup, your pet's energy needs are twice that of an adult dog. In fact, young puppies need 50 to 100 Calories per pound of body weight each day compared to 33 to 45 Calories for an active house dog. For this reason, Purina Puppy Foods are

high in protein, fat and contain all essential vitamins and minerals.

Proper feeding habits are normally formed during your pup's first six months. Take care to promote good eating habits and routines for your pet. There are, of course, special feeding conditions. Sick puppies should sometimes be fed often. Puppies kept in unheated kennels during winter weather need more food than those with warm kennels. On the other hand, puppies living in the house, and those difficult to housebreak, can be fed once a day.

If you prefer to feed your pup his ration dry, the food can be placed in a pan alongside another pan containing water and the dog will eat when he is hungry. The dry ration will then be available to the dog at all times. Dry puppy food is also an important part of your pet's diet because it helps to promote healthy gums and teeth.

Feeding Purina Puppy Foods wet, though, is recommended for young puppies because research shows they grow faster because they eat more. Add only enough water to moisten the food, not enough to make it mushy.

Keep feeding the special puppy food for his first *full* year, but, when the time comes to change to adult food, take care to change gradually. Accomplish the change by mixing the two foods and slowly increasing the amount of the new dog food.

Vitamin And Mineral Supplements

Although many vitamin and mineral supplements are marketed, they are not necessary when well-balanced rations are being fed. In fact, their use should be discouraged except as directed by your veterinarian, since it is possible to feed too many vitamins and minerals, which can be toxic or cause a nutritional imbalance.

Feeding Field Dogs

When dogs are in training, or actually are hunting, they use up tremendous amounts of energy. For example, some hard-working field dogs would lose weight since they sometimes expend more energy than they normally can take in during a day. Under these circumstances, the feeding program of High Protein Dog Meal can be supplemented by the addition of meat, which increases their appetite and increases their caloric

intake. High quality fresh or canned meat is normally an excellent source of protein and fat. Usually, one part of meat is added to four parts of dry ration.

Dogs should be worked regularly to reach maximum efficiency. Research has shown that dogs work more efficiently when fed lightly before periods of hard work.

Fat is the most concentrated source of energy—a small amount added to the ration will sometimes increase both feed intake and palatability. Most commercial rations have ample added fat. If it is necessary for fat to be added, lard, bacon grease or corn oil are good sources.

"Don'ts" Of Feeding Dogs

Modern dog foods are so good that most dogs live better than do their owners. So don't destroy the balance of a dog food— that has been made after generations of research—by adding bulky vegetables.

Don't feed bones. Some can splinter and may puncture the throat or digestive tract. Others can cause impaction in the intestines, bringing serious illness or death.

Leave human baby foods for babies unless your veterinarian recommends them as a temporary special diet. Don't give your dog raw eggs since they contain an enzyme, avidin, that destroys the vitamin biotin. Don't give milk to adult dogs since it has a tendency to cause diarrhea. Small puppies may also respond to milk in the same way. If so, remove milk and feed puppy food only.

Don't experiment with feeding a sick dog. Rely on your veterinarian for advice.

Don't feel you must feed table scraps or mix them into your pet's dinner of commercial dog food. All Purina dog food products are completely balanced in themselves to provide everything your pet needs.

Don't overfeed your dog. An overweight dog may be less active, more prone to certain health problems, and may have a shorter life span than a dog that is maintained at normal weight.

How to Housebreak Your Puppy

Several years ago a national magazine stated that you should not expect to housebreak your dog before it is seven to eight months old. Under the system outlined here, a puppy of six to eight weeks can be housebroken in a week or less. That is, any mistakes the dog makes after a week will be your mistakes.

Housebreaking depends upon the million-of-years-old instinct of the den dwellers to keep their beds clean. A horse or a canary is not a den dweller. One is a prairie animal; the other is a free-flying tree dweller. Neither needs to be housebroken in his natural habitat and neither can be under conditions man imposes upon him. But dogs and cats can be—quite easily. You simply make use of their ancient instinct and create a sort of home den for them.

The secret is to construct a box which will have a door or lid on it, with adequate ventilation holes. The box should be big enough for the puppy to turn about in, and even to lie at full length, but no larger. The lid, or door, is required because any puppy worth his salt can climb out of most boxes. Moreover, the box without a lid or door is an open invitation for the puppy to try to get out. He will cry continuously if he can't make it.

The reason for this box is that any puppy will respect his bed. He will not make a mess in his bed and then sleep in it. Now he might get caught the first night, but he won't the second. However, if the box is so large that he can relieve himself in one end and sleep in the other, he will do so.

It is a good idea to have the box larger than you will need at first, since this will allow for growth of the puppy. Or you can cut grooves in the sides and make a partition which can be moved farther back to enlarge the puppy's bed.

Bedding for the box can be plain newspaper laid flat. At first, you may think this cruel. But puppies usually scratch a blanket into a lump, then are uncomfortable trying to sleep on it. The paper is disposable, too.

You should have this box made before you get your puppy. Then you are ready for him. Remember that on the very first day it is important to start giving your puppy all his naps in the box. Little puppies play hard, then require a lot of naps, which should always be taken in the box. By night, the puppy already has the idea that the box is his bed. So you'll have less crying during the night.

Now your procedure is as follows. When the puppy awakens from his nap, you immediately lift him out of the box and carry him outside to a spot which you previously have selected and prepared. This spot is prepared by mopping up his first mistake and anchoring the rag in that spot. The puppy smells where he has been before, or thinks he has, and gets the idea immediately.

Play always excites a puppy and makes him want to urinate. You must always take him to his spot before and after play; always when he awakens from a nap; and always the first thing in the morning and the last thing at night. You must never "just put him out." Instead, you must take him to his spot, urge him to go, and compliment him when he does. Within a week, you'll have him going on command.

Of course, there are times when he'll make a mistake in the house. In those cases, scold him and show him where he should have gone. Except after a mistake, always wait until he does relieve himself before bringing him back into the house.

Thousands of people who read such instructions as these decide that the weather is too cold, or it is raining, and the puppy will catch cold. Usually they are making excuses for themselves. By the time puppies are weaned they have good thick fur. That fur makes an insulation blanket of heat between the dog's skin and the cold or rain, so he won't catch cold in the

short time he's out to relieve himself. He's much more likely to get it over with in a hurry so he can get back into the house.

With the possible exceptions of the toy breeds or if outdoor training is impractical at first because of apartment dwelling, illness, or other reasons, it is not recommended to housebreak a puppy to relieve himself on paper or to go into the basement to do it. To do this is to corrupt his cleanliness instinct. Many dogs cannot be retrained to go outside, so if you start them on paper you may be in for trouble.

Puppy's box should be placed in the kitchen. That's because the kitchen is the most "used" room in the house. Moreover, puppy's play hours should be in the kitchen until you can trust him. The kitchen probably has a tile or linoleum floor. This is easy to clean.

A puppy has a "nose brain," as we told you earlier. If he smells urine odor, he's likely to want to use that spot again. So when he makes a mistake, wash the linoleum with soap and water several times. Then sprinkle a drop or two of ammonia solution on the wet spot and rub it about. This will discourage the puppy from using that area again.

The housebreaking box you have prepared can—and should—serve as a permanent home for the dog. Your puppy will come to think of it—or a larger edition—as his personal home. He'll prefer it to any other bed. Moreover, if you've taught him as a little puppy to sleep in the box quietly, you'll have no later trouble. Literally thousands of dogs that sleep on their owners' beds, on the davenport, or in the bedroom, develop personality traits. They howl when left alone, or they tear things up in spite.

If your dog has an outside run or pen, a manure disposal pit can be an ideal place for the disposal of droppings. For a single dog a hole a foot in diameter and 3 inches deep will last for quite a while. For several dogs a buried barrel without ends works well. A plywood cover will keep dogs and children out.

Summary

Use a dog's ancient instinct to keep his bed clean. Do this by building a box bed, with strong door or lid and adequate ventilation. This should be one of your own projects. Puppy will want to keep the bed box, or a larger one, as a permanent home. If you arrange this, you'll avoid later personality problems and problems with guests who don't like dogs. Mistakes made after the first three days in your home will probably be yours rather than puppy's. Don't use the excuse that the weather is too cold to take puppy out. Housebreak toy dogs—and toy dogs only—to use newspaper placed in a certain area of the house.

Your Dog's Health

The first rule in taking care of your dog is: When your dog is sick, take him to a veterinarian. Use with caution advice of friends or people who are supposed to be "old, experienced dog breeders." Only a veterinarian is qualified to diagnose trouble and prescribe treatment.

However, it is your job to *keep* your dog from getting sick. Let us assume you start with a puppy. You should know something about "shots," worm medicines, flea powders, and poisons.

While a puppy is nursing, it may receive protective antibodies in its mother's milk. As soon as the puppy is weaned, this natural immunity will begin to disappear and may be gone within two weeks. Many puppies are susceptible to diseases at this young age. Your veterinarian may prescribe a vaccination program beginning at 6 to 8 weeks. Contact him immediately.

Distemper, hepatitis and leptospirosis are common and serious diseases which destroy many pets each year. Rabies is also a threat which should be guarded against in rural as well as metropolitan areas because of the possible chance of exposure to bites of affected animals and vaccinations are required by law in most of the U.S.

The only satisfactory method of protecting your dog is by vaccination. Your veterinarian may want to give your puppy immediate temporary protection at the time of purchase with a "puppy shot" of antiserum which contains antibodies against distemper, hepatitis and leptospirosis as well as some of the other common diseases. Vaccinations provide long term immunity and most puppies will be started on a series of vaccinations on their first visit to the veterinarian. Booster vaccines are then advisable on a regular basis for adult dogs.

Distemper

In its initial phase, the symptoms of distemper may be difficult to differentiate from other disease conditions. One should be alerted to the probable presence of this virus infection if the dog shows an elevation of temperature, a lack of appetite and evidence of depression. When such symptoms develop get the dog to a veterinarian and don't wait until there is evidence of a discharge from the eyes and nose, a severe diarrhea, pneumonia, or convulsive attacks. The quicker that treatment is initiated under the direction of a veterinarian the greater the chance of recovery. Dogs which recover from distemper are usually considered to be permanently immune but to be safe the dog should have a yearly booster.

There are several different types of vaccines to help prevent distemper. Their choice and their program of use should rest with the veterinarian and will, of course, be based upon his experience in controlling this disease in the community. A few general comments on the subject of distemper vaccination may, however, be in order.

The immunity response to the vaccination affords a high level of protection for about a year at which time the protection will begin to disappear. Thus a distemper booster should be given every year for maximum protection.

In summary, there are three major points to stress. (1) Puppy shots at the time of purchase may be used to provide immediate but temporary protection, (2) begin a vaccination program at 6 to 8 weeks of age and (3) see your veterinarian immediately and follow his recommendations closely.

Hepatitis

This is a virus infection which, as the name implies, primarily affects the liver tissue. This disease began to be recognized only about 25 years ago. Dogs of middle age are usually not seriously affected but puppies and aged dogs often die from this virus infection. In the initial stage the symptoms such as sudden rise and fall in temperature, impairment of appetite and depression are almost identical with those of distemper. There may even be a serous discharge from the eyes and nose. There may be some pain to pressure over the abdomen and vomition. Uncontrolled bleeding or skin bruises are other signs of hepatitis.

Hepatitis can be prevented by vaccination. The vaccine may be given at the same time as the anti-distemper vaccine. A point to remember is that the virus of hepatitis (and distemper) is voided in the urine and that both diseases can be present at the same time. The virus causing hepatitis in the dog is not transmissable to man. Viral hepatitis of people is caused by a completely different virus.

Leptospirosis

This acute infectious disease of dogs is spread through contact of the mouth or nasal mucous membranes with the urine of either an infected dog or rat. Within 5 to 15 days after such exposure the disease begins with a sudden rise of body temperature, weakness, refusal to eat and vomiting. These symptoms are not unlike those of the initial phase of distemper or hepatitis, however, within a day or two there is usually a sharp drop in temperature, breathing is labored and one may observe some evidence of stiffness, particularly in the hind legs. Vaccination is recommended for prevention of this increasingly important disease.

Rabies

The virus infection is transmitted through the bite of affected animals and may affect a great many species including man. Since the disease is transmissible to man its control is a public health problem and dog populations are, therefore, subject to regulatory measures covering restriction of movement, quarantine and vaccination programs. Although the probability of your dog being exposed to this disease will vary greatly by areas, it is recommended that you have your dog vaccinated. In many areas rabies vaccinations are required by law. Consult your veterinarian as to the age that this vaccination program should be started.

Parainfluenza

A virus disease spread in the air, it affects mainly the upper respiratory tract. It is commonly known as "kennel cough". The dog may have a mild fever, nasal discharge, mild tonsilitis and will usually demonstrate a series of harsh nonproductive coughs ending with a gag or retch.

Complications follow if secondary infections by other organisms occur. A vaccine is available at your veterinary hospital.

Internal Parasites (Worms)

It is difficult to rear puppies free of worms. The type of worm may vary from area to area, but worms are a common problem and all puppies should be checked for them at the time of purchase. This check requires laboratory and microscopic examination of a stool sample from the pet and should be done by a veterinarian, who will want to determine if parasites are present before planning a vaccination program.

The symptoms, if any, which the parasitized dog may show will vary with the degree and type of infestation. Once the veterinarian has determined which type of parasite is present,

31

he will prescribe the preferred medicine indicated for treatment of your dog.

Roundworms

Roundworms are one of the most common intestinal parasites. Although the infested dog (especially older) will often show no symptoms, a stool check will tell if the dog is infested, and there are several medications available for treatment of the problem.

Hookworms

Hookworms take a deadly toll of puppies. Often, the puppies get them from their mothers before birth. Some may die within two weeks; others will begin to show serious illness at five or six weeks. Again, a stool check is required to verify infestation, and the veterinarian will want to prescribe medication and start treatment as quickly as possible.

Whipworms

A stool check is also required to verify whipworm infestation. These worms are difficult to eliminate. They are much more apt to strike kennel dogs than pet dogs, but they do reach both. Work is currently under way to develop more effective medications for the treatment of whipworms, and it is hoped these will be available in the not too distant future.

Tapeworms

Tapeworms are common in older dogs. At one stage in their life cycles tapeworms are carried in fleas, which live on dogs, cats and humans. If a dog swallows a flea, the tapeworm eggs can hatch and develop. Other species are transmitted when a dog ingests tapeworm cysts located in other animals, i.e. by eating uncleaned rabbits, sheep or deer carcasses.

Tapeworm segments break off and are eliminated with the dog's stools, in which you can observe the small, rectangular segments, providing proof of infestation. Tapeworms can live in dogs for years without doing serious harm. But they do irritate the intestine, eat food the dog should be getting, and if the dog gets sick they can mean the difference between life and death.

Heartworms

Canine heartworm infection, which has been a serious problem for years in the southern states, is becoming very important in the midwest and has been reported in all 50 states. Adult heartworms live in or near the heart, causing an elevation in blood pressure and resulting in damage to the surrounding muscles and blood vessels. If both male and female adults are present, microscopic larvae called microfilariae are born. These microfilariae, circulating in the blood of a dog for one to two years (possibly causing damage to the kidneys and other body tissues) are picked up by a biting mosquito. Here they develop after two weeks into microfilariae capable of infecting a healthy dog. If the mosquito then feeds on another dog, the microfilariae invade the new dog's body.

Following several molts in the dog, the microfilariae mature into adult heartworms, completing the life cycle. If your dog shows signs of tiring on excercise, gradual weight loss, weakness, coughing or heavy breathing, see your veterinarian at once for a physical exam. The presence of heartworms may be the cause of his general unthriftiness. Your veterinarian's recommendations for treatment should be followed closely, and mosquito populations should be kept under control as much as possible.

External Parasites

Worms are internal parasites. External parasites are fleas, lice, ticks, and mites. There are many powders on the market

that will kill fleas, mites, and lice. Some may even kill ticks. But there are also special preparations for ticks alone. Fleas not only make your dog's life miserable, but act to bring on more formidable problems such as tapeworms and skin allergies.

The important thing is to use them regularly. They come as aerosol sprays, powders, soaps and shampoos, and liquids that can be rubbed into the coat. The liquids and aerosols, and even the shampoos, may be flammable and are dangerous if the user is smoking or is using them near a stove or heater. Consult your veterinarian for an appropriate recommendation.

First Aid For Your Dog

Most dogs, especially a puppy, are as curious, heedless and impulsive as children, and can get into just as much trouble. Although the veterinarian should always be your first consultant, knowing a little first aid can help a dog in minor mishaps, and in some cases even save his life.

Again, prevention is better than any cure, so try to keep your house and grounds pet safe. Keep sharp, pointed objects, soft rubber or plastic toys, painted toys and sharp bones out of reach. Lock up all medicines, soaps and insecticides. Keep a small medicine box for your dog including:

■ *A rectal thermometer and lubricant*
■ *Adhesive tape and gauze (for bandaging)*
■ *Burn medicine prescribed by the veterinarian*
■ *Boric acid or collyrium (eye wash)*
■ *Kaopectate for diarrhea*
■ *Spirits of ammonia for shock treatment*
■ *Mustard powder or table salt as emetics (induce vomiting)*
■ *Activated charcoal for poison antidote (call veterinarian)*
■ *Mild laxative (i.e., Milk of Magnesia)*

Serious Accident

■ *Call your veterinarian.*
■ *Do not move the dog.*
■ *Try to stop bleeding.*
■ *Keep him warm and quiet.*

Tying The Mouth Shut

When dogs are in great pain, they are apt to bite out unseeingly. To prevent being bitten in such cases—as when giving first aid to a dog hit by a car — wrap a strip of cloth around the muzzle. Tie it over the muzzle then under the chin and then back of the ears. He will be unable to get it off. If you tie it only under the chin, it will slip off.

Note: If the dog *must* be moved, do *not* lift him in your arms, but transfer him to a blanket or any solid object which can be used as a stretcher and carried with as little vibration as possible.

External Bleeding

Only profuse bleeding, which might be arterial, is dangerous. Apply pressure pad or bandage directly to wound and hold until you can reach the veterinarian.

Symptoms of Illness

After watching your dog for awhile, you should be able to tell whether he is in good health, is ailing slightly, or is coming down with something really serious. Loss of appetite is an early sign. Refusal to eat can be a strong symptom. The lower eyelid may hang down slightly, showing the red membrane. The coat may have a harsh feel and a dead texture, both to the eye and hand.

Mucus in the stools and traces of blood are signs that the dog is not well. A potbelly, yet with skinniness elsewhere, is a sign of trouble. Lack of interest is another. Hiding in dark places may be a serious sign that the dog is sick.

The temperature of the dog's nose is *not* an indication that a dog is sick. Any discharge from the nose or eyes is a command for you to visit the veterinarian with your dog.

COMMON HEALTH PROBLEMS

Poisonings

Modern man is having an ever more serious war against some insects, fungi, bacteria, rats, and mice. He fights these with an increasing array of poisons. Many of these poisons work for a time, then the insects become immune to them. So new poisons must be invented. The dog is in constant danger from such poisons since they are used on lawns, shrubs, gardens, and fruit trees.

Your first concern must be to keep your dog from getting poisoned. Keep him away from lawns and gardens where insecticides have been used. Never place rat poison where the dog can get it or where the rat can carry it into the open. If you are putting out rat poison keep a careful lookout for dead or dying rats which your dog might get and eat.

POISONS

Pyrophosphates. These include Pestox III, TEPP, Malathion, Parathion, and others. They are absorbed through the skin. Symptoms are pin-point pupils, heavy salivation (slobbering), violent cramps, respiratory spasms, eye watering, and muscular twitching.

ANTU. This is a rat poison. Symptoms are gastric distress, difficult breathing, a bubbling sound in the lungs, prostration, and coma.

Arsenic. It is used as a rat poison, dip, spray, or as a syrup for insects. Early symptoms are acute abdominal pain, diarrhea (often bloody), and rear-end paralysis.

Warfarin. One of the best of the new rat poisons. It is not supposed to hurt pets but it sometimes does. Symptoms are those of severe shock, an abrupt drop in blood pressure, a cold body, weak breathing, a fast heart rate and internal or external bleeding.

Red Squill. This is another rat poison which is not supposed to injure dogs. If it is placed in a carrier so that it passes the stomach, then the dog is in trouble. If it reaches him in normal form, the dog vomits and that saves him. It kills rats because they cannot vomit. Symptoms are severe pain which causes the dog to yelp if touched about the chest or abdomen. It also causes the dog to stagger.

> **If your dog swallows poison, be able to tell the veterinarian what kind or type of poison it is. This will give him the key to what antidote to use.**

Burns

A good first treatment for burns is to apply cold running water. If the burn is not too serious, nonprescription burn medications can be applied. For more severe burns contact your veterinarian.

Shock

This dangerous condition whether from injury or trauma calls for immediate action. (Symptoms are prostration, "glazed" eye, cold body, feeble pulse and shallow breathing.) Cover the dog with a blanket, plus heating pad or hot water bottle. Be sure his head is lower than his body. Briefly hold open bottle of spirits of ammonia under his nostrils. Call veterinarian for other instructions.

Heat Prostration

It is sad this situation should ever occur, because it is usually through ignorance that pet owners allow their dogs to become overheated to this extent. Remember, if you're hot, he's hot, and act accordingly. *Never, never* leave your dog in your closed car in hot weather, and if he is left outside be sure shade is available.

However, when heat prostration does occur, symptoms are: difficulty in breathing, loud panting, weakness, and even unconsciousness. Try to cool off the dog quickly by sponging him with cold water in a quiet, shady spot. You can also try spirits of ammonia if available, holding open bottle under nostrils. Call your veterinarian, but *remember* heat prostration can be totally prevented if you protect your dog in the first place.

Insect Stings

These are usually minor, and if anything is used, a pain-killing ointment or bicarbonate of soda compress should help. A good emergency measure is to cake the sting with mud. *However,* if severe allergic reaction should occur, or the dog goes into shock, follow previous treatment and consult veterinarian.

Skunk

When a dog receives a direct hit of skunk musk it must be a most unpleasant experience for him and his owner ... and before you can both inhabit the same house again *deodorizing* is the only answer. We still recommend the old remedy — tomato juice. Either bathe him in it or sponge him until the skunky odor subsides, then follow with a good dog soap and warm water bath. (Be careful of chilling!) A strong spray in the eyes can cause temporary blindness. Wash out your dog's eyes with mild boric acid solution or collyrium. If severe, call your veterinarian.

How To Give Medicines

During your life with your dog, your veterinarian will give you pills or medicines to give to him. So you should learn how to do this. It is not difficult.

Liquids: Usually the veterinarian will give you a small vial holding an ounce or so of liquid. Make your dog sit. Then pull out his cheek to make a pouch. Put the vial into the cheek pouch and let the medicine drain into the throat. The dog will have to swallow it. Be sure to keep the dog's head horizontal to the floor.

Pills: Make the dog sit. Grasp his upper jaw with one hand, pressing the lips against the teeth until he opens his mouth. Use the longest finger of your other hand to force the pill far enough down his throat so that he has to swallow it. Hold the mouth closed for a moment, and stroke the throat from the outside until you are sure he has swallowed it. Large pills can be moistened with mineral oil, butter or margarine for easier swallowing.

Summary

The major health problems of your dog are best handled by your veterinarian. But you should learn how to recognize signs of illness, to give first aid when necessary, to deworm, and give other pills and medicines as the veterinarian may prescribe. Keep poisons away from your dog; go farther in protecting your dog from them than the label prescribes. See that your dog is vaccinated against distemper, hepatitis, and leptospirosis. Keep your dog confined, but also have him protected by rabies vaccine.

Have booster shots given as suggested by your veterinarian, periodically during the dog's life and before going to dog shows.

Grooming Your Dog

Your most intimate relationship with your dog is when you groom him. As we have pointed out, the dog enjoys doing things for others—whether dogs or humans. He's a sociable animal. But doing things for others should never be a "one-way street." He likes for you to do things for him, too. And he will never be happier than when you are grooming him.

Moreover, it is while grooming your dog that you best learn whether he is sick or well, whether he is prospering or is lagging in health and development. For instance, many a dog owner has failed to notice such things as lice and ticks, just because he has failed to groom his dog.

You will hear it said that dogs should not have a bath until they are a year old. This is plain "bunk." Puppies may get dirty and need baths. When they need them, they should have them, unless they are sick. The important thing is *how* you give the bath, and with *what* kind of soap.

Years ago, a flea soap was apt to be a very strong soap, with flea-killing elements that tended to irritate the dog's skin. Today there are dozens of kinds of soaps and shampoos, many of which are as gentle as those used by humans. The flea-killing soaps are also mild.

For dogs, there are specially made shampoos (including those in aerosol containers), dry baths, and plain bar soaps. In addition, there are soaps for humans that are both bactericidal and deodorant. Chances are, you use one yourself. Such soaps will do for your dog. Remember to rinse well with clean warm water to remove all shampoo or soap.

The dog's fur holds heat in or keeps it out. In other words, it is an insulating blanket against rapid changes in weather. When you bathe a dog you temporarily destroy this insulating blanket. The result is, the dog shivers.

You should bathe your dog in water of a temperature of about 100 degrees, which comes close to his body temperature. After the bath, dry him with a towel. You can pin a fresh towel about him to help him until he restores that insulation blanket; you can dry him with mother's electric hair dryer, or you can put him under a heat lamp. Play always helps. Do not let puppy out of doors. He may catch cold or he may roll in dirt and destroy results of the bath.

Combs help to remove dirt particles. The finer combs will even bring out fleas and lice. Sometimes they are used to bring out water after the dog's bath. Combing and brushing will help to prevent hair mats or balls, will distribute hair oil, and will help to make the healthy coat glisten. Combing also helps to keep the hair in place.

Many people think combs will pull out dead and shedding hair. Here, for the most part, combs fail. When dogs are shedding, the best way to remove hair is to get the dog between your legs, massage his coat and skin with your hands to loosen hair, then stroke from head to foot with the palms of your hands. If you do this twice a day in the back yard during the shedding season, you'll have very few shedding problems.

It is best to cut out hair mats. This can be done with scissors or with a trimming knife or plucking razor. The latter is the perfect instrument for removing burrs. It takes out the burrs with little pain, and in a third the time required if you use a comb.

Much of your grooming should take place on a steady table or workbench. In this way, you accustom the dog to being on a table and to being worked on, on a table. This means you'll have less trouble at the veterinarian's. Such grooming experience also teaches the dog to take whatever is necessary without growling or biting.

While you have the dog on the table, examine his toenails. If they are so long that they're flattening out the foot, cut or file them back to the quick. Dogs probably resent work on their nails more than anything else. If you start while he's young, you'll teach your puppy to accept this grooming. If overly difficult, ask your veterinarian to trim the nails. He'll be happy to help.

Check the ears. Trim away excess hair which might prevent air from getting into the ear canal. Look for mites and louse eggs—minute specks stuck to the hair. If the ear canal is red, inflamed, and hot, or has a foul odor, it is best to see your veterinarian. Be warned in advance that too much interference with the ear canals can bring permanent trouble.

If yours is a hunting dog, check him after each workout for burrs between the toes, and under the legs, near the body; and for weed seeds in the eye pockets. In dry weather, even dust from plants can cause eye irritation. Use plain water, boric acid, or get a bland solution from your veterinarian.

Summary

Give your dog a bath when he needs it. Just use common sense and care in drying and warming him again. Keep the bath-water temperature at 100°F. Use brush and comb for grooming, but use the hands to loosen shedding hair. Do much of your grooming on a table, so the dog will be used to it before going to the veterinarian's. Check hunting dogs for burrs between the toes and under the legs, near the body. Be sure the eyes are clear of dust or weed seeds.

Puppies on the Way

Well, it happened. A litter of puppies is on the way. Whether the result of careful study of pedigrees and blood lines to select the right mate or personal selection of that handsome black dog in the next block, you're in for an interesting experience.

Let's assume you are a complete novice. You will welcome some basic information. The only time your female will show an interest in her sex life is during her heat period. This should first occur between the age of six months and one year and every six months thereafter. Only during heat can she be bred and conceive. Should your female come in heat much under one year of age, she is usually not mature enough for breeding. Wait until her second or a later period. Generally speaking, about 12-18 months of age for small breeds and 14-24 months for larger and slower maturing breeds would be ideal.

The heat cycle usually lasts 18 to 21 days, with a certain period within the cycle when she can be bred with the greatest chances of becoming pregnant. From about the 10th to 14th day your female will become very interested in receiving male dog attentions, so care must be taken to be sure none but the selected sire can get to her.

For healthy and vigorous puppies, it is extremely important that the mother be in top physical condition. This includes not being overweight or showing symptoms of a hormone imbalance. Excessive weight can cause difficulty at whelping time and cause small litters. If worms are present, she should be wormed under the supervision of your veterinarian—not later than two or three weeks after pregnancy begins. Be certain that she is free of lice, ticks and fleas and has been immunized against distemper, hepatitis, influenza and leptospirosis before becoming pregnant. Temporary resistance to diseases will be passed on to the puppies in the milk of the mother.

After the honeymoon, allow her normal activities. As she puts on weight, she will be less anxious to romp and play. Whatever happens, don't allow her to cease all activities. Without exercise she may become overweight making whelping more difficult. Gestation lasts roughly nine weeks, although you should be ready for the puppies' arrival from the 60th day on.

From the fifth week on, don't allow her to dash up and down stairs or jump on or off furniture. But exercise on a scaled-down basis must continue until whelping time. Take care she doesn't become chilled when wet.

A whelping box should be used during birth and nursing. A good one is closed in on three sides with an entrance cut in the fourth. An entrance barrier, four to six inches high will make it easy for the mother to step in but impossible for the pups to get out. The box should be large enough so she can stretch out at full length on her side with room to spare for whelping. Whelping box plans are available from the Purina Pet Care Center, Ralston Purina Company, St. Louis, Mo. 63188.

A railing around the inside of the whelping box, three or four inches high, will prevent the newborn pups from getting mashed by the mother. Keep room temperature at least 70°F. to prevent the puppies from becoming chilled. Fifty percent of puppy losses are attributable to chilling.

Incidentally, accustom your female to her whelping box several days before her puppies are due by inserting her regular mattress or blanket. She'll feel at home when it's time for the puppies to arrive. Replace her regular mattress or blanket just prior to whelping with several layers of flat newspaper. Place the whelping box away from family traffic pattern. She should have a quiet spot to be alone with her babies.

Two or three days before the puppies are due, your pet

should definitely present a sagging appearance. Her breasts will become enlarged and reddish and she will be short of breath and pant heavily. The surest sign that it's time for arrival is when she begins to shred the newspapers to build a nest. Keep quiet and leave her alone. Mother Nature will take over.

The first labor pains may make her uncomfortable and she will lie on her side and strain for delivery. Between labor periods, expect more panting and heavy water consumption. Let her walk around. She will return to her whelping box in plenty of time. Usually there will be a discharge of mucus, nature's lubricant, just before the first puppy begins to arrive.

Each puppy will arrive enclosed in a somewhat transparent membrane sac. Although the sacs are tough, they are occasionally ruptured during delivery. First you will see a bulge, then the whitish membrane sac. Immediately you will see the puppy, then the umbilical cord with attached afterbirth. The female will tear away the sac, bite off the umbilical cord and eat the afterbirth. This is perfectly normal. She will clean the puppy's nostrils of mucus and lick the little fellow dry from stem to stern. If she seems rough, she is just starting the puppy's breathing and circulation. On rare occasions the mother will not open the sac. On such occasions the owner should quickly, but carefully, slit the sac, removing the puppy so it will not smother.

If a newborn puppy doesn't start breathing immediately and the mother appears to be neglecting it, rub him vigorously in a soft towel. The puppy should respond with cries which is a good sign. Replace him near his mother immediately to encourage her to begin maternal care.

If the umbilical cord is not cut, tie a sterile thread about one inch from the body, nip off with a dull pair of scissors and swab with iodine.

Some females will not care for their pups and resent outside assistance. You can overcome this by leaving one or two puppies with her while caring for another. Resist the urge to help unless a puppy is in danger. Your good intentions may be more disturbing than helpful.

Puppies are born with their eyes closed and will remain so for about ten days. They should not be exposed to bright sunlight for several days thereafter.

Make certain all afterbirths have been expelled. A retained afterbirth usually means serious difficulties for the new mother. The dark red discharge after whelping usually means all afterbirths have been expelled. Consult your veterinarian if vaginal discharges persist for 2-3 days and the female drinks large quantities of water. Do not attempt to treat the female yourself.

Make a rule—and stick to it—no visitors allowed in the nursery for the first three days. Keep children away until your pet is sure her babies are okay. Only one visitor at a time and caution them to be very careful of the new arrivals. Some females become very upset with strangers handling their pups.

The greatest puppy mortality occurs at birth or within the first week. Watch to see each gets his share of food and is growing normally. Help the little fellow who seems to be crowded out. It may be necessary to guide him to a nursing station frequently.

During the latter stages of pregnancy the prospective mother's daily food intake will normally increase about 20%. If she is being fed a completely balanced ration, such as Purina® Dog Chow®, Purina High Protein® Dog Meal or Chuck Wagon® then she is receiving adequate nutrition.

Directly after the puppies have arrived, she will not be too interested in food. As her appetite returns, feed her all she wants. She needs energy for her own body to return to normal and to supply the milk.

It is most important that the puppies receive plenty of milk from their mother. They will whine almost constantly if they do not get the milk. If she is not producing enough milk, supplement her Purina® Dog Chow®, Chuck Wagon® or High Protein Dog Meal with 10-20% raw meat. If she isn't able to nurse her puppies, see your veterinarian immediately.

At 3 to 3½ weeks of age, the puppies will begin to nibble the mother's food and should be allowed all they will eat. Purina puppy foods are designed especially for young, growing puppies up to a year old. Puppies need and burn up three times the energy of a grown dog and require 17½% more protein. Purina puppy foods (mixed one part warm water to two parts puppy food) provides your puppy all he needs in a dinner he will thrive on and love.

Spaying and Neutering— the Facts of Life

If healthy, the neutering of your female or male dog is a relatively safe operation, and is usually recommended by your veterinarian unless you intend to breed your dog. Sometimes the operation disturbs the dog owner psychologically or emotionally far more than the dog, who quickly recovers and becomes an even better pet.

Female Dog

If your dog is a female, you have a special consideration. The female dog (bitch) matures more rapidly than the male dog, usually coming into breeding age at about seven months old, although she may reach breeding age as early as five months old. When she is in heat (twice a year for about three weeks at a time), male dogs will be constantly under foot, fighting, running and annoying you and your neighbors in their attempts to court her. She is capable of producing dozens of puppies in her lifetime, so unless you are breeding your dog purposely, with ready sales in the offing, you will have the responsibility of finding homes for all of her offspring. If you do not welcome that job, you should seriously consider having your female spayed.

Spaying (Ovario-hysterectomy)

Many veterinarians feel that the ideal age for spaying is about five to six months old, before the puppy has had her first seasonal period. If you would like your bitch to have a litter or two before having her spayed, you can still have the operation performed safely at a later age. Usually it is not recommended that a female be mated until she is one year old. (See chapter Puppies on the Way.)

In a healthy dog the operation of spaying involves a general anesthetic, abdominal surgery and the hospitalization of your pet. For the first few days the dog is home, care should be taken so she does not break open the incision. The younger female dog usually heals faster than the older one as might be expected.

In addition, spaying will probably lengthen the life of your pet for she will have fewer health problems. For instance, the spayed dog does not develop pyometritis, a uterine infection not uncommon in unspayed, middle-aged or older females, which may require surgical treatment at a time when she is quite ill. The spayed bitch is also less likely to develop breast tumors which often occur as she gets older, especially if she has raised several litters.

The alternative to spaying your dog is to keep a close watch on her for the entire time she is in heat. You may decide to put her in a good boarding kennel during this time. This will eliminate the possibility of a litter of unwanted, mixed-breed puppies, and the problem of being besieged by male dogs. Your neighbors will deeply appreciate your thoughtfulness.

If you do not wish to board your dog in a kennel, then you should plan to keep her in the house almost constantly during this time. When it's necessary to take her out, be sure to keep her on a short leash and take along a cane to frighten off male dogs. Or better still, drive to some secluded area or vacant lot, where you can let her exercise, but never off the leash. Only when her heat period is over and she is no longer attractive to males should you relax your vigilance.

Neutering Or Castration

Neutering or castration of a male dog is an operation which may be performed at any time, but usually after the age of four months. This operation will require general anesthesia and usually brief hospitalization.

After he has had the operation your dog will make an even better pet. He will express his vitality in play ofter ceasing some of his male behavioral traits found to be embarrasing and unwanted. He will also stay at home more, decreasing his chances of being hurt or killed and less apt to damage a neighbor's personal property.

The Dog Owner's Responsibilities

Any person who owns a dog must realize that he or she has taken the welfare of a living animal as his or her responsibility. This is not a small matter. For aside from the question of the dog's happiness, there is the question of proper moral conduct on the owner's part. Thus, you have to feed and care for your dog properly. More than that, you must teach him proper manners. If you do not, you may have neighbor trouble. Both you and your dog will suffer.

When you get a dog, you should make up your mind that your dog will not be allowed to bark so much that he becomes a nuisance. He won't be allowed to roam the neighborhood and become a bum. He won't be permitted to annoy mail and delivery men, garbage collectors and meter readers.

You will learn ways to control your dog and to correct his bad habits in later chapters. It is necessary to stress here that proper dog control and the prevention and cure of bad habits are *your responsibilities,* if you are to become a good dog neighbor.

Every dog owner should learn the major dog laws of his state. Visit the library or discuss the subject with an attorney. If you live in a town or city, check the city code for local ordinances. This is one way to get a clearer understanding of your responsibilities as a dog owner and be a good dog neighbor.

In most parts of North America, it is required that you get your dog licensed. These license fees are an excise tax levied upon the dogs of the community or county. License-issuing agencies are required to keep records and to supply the dog owner with a license tag. This tag is designed to be placed on a dog's collar. It serves to identify the dog if he is picked up by police. But it also identifies him if he gets lost. So a dog license tag is good insurance for you. Remember, the tag is no good to you unless it is securely fastened to the dog's collar, and the dog must be wearing that collar.

Many parents will say: "I like a dog, but the city is no place for him." But the fact is that country dogs get into more trouble than do city dogs.

This brings up the fact that parents of dog-owning children also have responsibilities. Boys and girls and dogs go naturally together. They learn responsibility, mercy, and general good character. They learn proper dog care against the time when they themselves will be parents of children wanting dogs.

Dog laws usually place full responsibility upon the dog's owner for any damage the dog may do. This is another reason why you should decide before you get a dog that you are going to give it proper care.

If you live on a farm, you'll want to introduce your dog to such things as chickens and other livestock.

You won't want it chasing or killing your own or your neighbor's livestock. It is relatively simple to teach the dog not to do this. You simply take it, for instance, into the chicken yard. If it starts to chase the chickens, you jerk back on the leash sharply and say "No!" A few lessons are all he'll need.

You have a responsibility to keep your dog in good health, not only for his sake but for that of other dogs. You keep your own dog in good health so that he won't spread disease to other dogs. And you keep your dog at home where he belongs, so that there is less danger that he will become infected by sick animals in the neighborhood.

The Do's and Don'ts of Dog Ownership

DO ...

■ *teach your dog to be obedient and well-behaved*

■ *walk your dog on a leash and curb him when necessary*

■ *teach him to stay in your yard*

■ *train your dog to stay quietly within his kennel or crate while you are away*

■ *train your dog to walk quietly at heel on a loose leash*

DON'T ...

■ *let your dog roam the neighborhood*

■ *let your dog bark excessively*

■ *let your dog soil your neighbor's shrubbery or lawn, or tear up his flower garden*

50

■ *let your dog chase cars or bicycles*
■ *let your dog frighten or bite the postman, milkman, or other service people*
■ *let your leashed dog lunge at or jump on passers-by*
■ *let your dog howl for hours while you are gone*

Yard Manners

Even the friendliest of neighbors will be resentful and angry if the dog next door wanders unchecked all over their lawn, soils their yard, and tears up their lawn or flowers.

A dog isn't born with yard manners and probably has no idea the neighbors will object to his activities. Or if he knows from painful experience that they do, he doesn't understand why.

So the solution is up to you.

It's quite normal for a dog not to soil his own yard. So, unless you find an alternative, he'll go to the neighbor's lawn.

Teach your dog to use only a certain portion of your own yard—behind or beside the garage, or out behind the shrubbery. You can do this by placing some of his droppings there, then taking him to that spot when you know it is necessary. When he relieves himself there, praise him.

Meanwhile, spray any other yard spot he has used previously with a good commercial deodorant. The smell will keep your dog away from those areas, and he will start using the area you have chosen for him.

If you fence the area you have selected, you can leave your dog there for an hour or so at regular times each day.

To keep this area clean, droppings should be disposed of regularly. They can be placed in the street sewer or used in your garden as manure. Various scoop-type gadgets are sold which make it easy to pick up and dispose of the droppings.

Planned Pethood (5 minutes) Responsible dog ownership includes birth control. Using animated clay figures, this film reviews various problems of surplus and intact animals, and points out how surgical neutering can eliminate these problems, making life healthier for your dog and happier for your family.

Modern Talking Pictures Service
1687 Elmhurst Road
Elk Grove Village, IL 60007

How to Travel with Your Dog

It happens every year. Millions of vacationing and moving families face the question of "what to do about their pet."

If on vacation should you take him...or leave him? As a member of the family, your pet in entitled to share the fun of traveling. On the other hand, some pets can take all the pleasure out of a trip. Think before you decide. A week or two in a clean, well-run boarding kennel might be your dog's idea of a perfect vacation.

A dog should be thoroughly familiar with riding in a car before you consider taking him on a long trip. After a few rides around town most dogs overcome their motion sickness and begin to enjoy riding with the family. If your pet does not travel well and continues to get sick or restless, consider a boarding kennel. Don't take a carsick or unhappy dog on a trip. Both you and your pet will be miserable.

But suppose you decide to take him along. Do you know the responsibility that goes with traveling with your dog? A first step should be to tuck a $10 bill in an envelope as a deposit for hotel or motel owners to guarantee your dog's good manners. Anytime a hotel or motel refuses to accept dogs it is usually the result of an irresponsible previous dog-owning guest. Make your reservations well in advance, advising that you will have a dog with you. This could save much time and aggravation. Automobile Clubs and motel guides often list hotels and motels which accept dogs.

Take along your pet's own bowl. Use it for water and mixing his food. He will have an added feeling of security using his regular bowl. If you feed a dry dog food, your feeding problem is solved. Mix about six parts Purina® Dog Chow® or four parts High Protein Dog Meal with one part warm water, and mix to a crumbly texture. There is no waste to this method. Also, try not to feed your pet for six or more hours prior to traveling. Most dogs travel better on this feeding schedule.

Your dog should wear two collars. One light chain-choke collar and a leather collar, rolled or flat. Put an identification tag on one and your local dog license on the other. Even if one collar is lost, he could be identified by the other.

Take along a square of old blanket or his sleeping pad. This is your dog's travel bed in the car and motel. After you've shown him a couple of times, he'll understand.

A can of flea powder is a must. Your pet may start out without a single flea, but he could pick some up along the way. You don't want fleas in your car, and the hotel or motel doesn't want them either.

Some dogs insist on hanging their heads out the windows. Don't permit this. Bits of grit may be driven into the eyes. In any case, the dog may get nasal and eye passage inflammation just from the wind. Keep him in his place and close the windows part way to discourage him.

If you will be traveling between several states, check with your veterinarian or humane society to find whether health certificates and proof of rabies vaccination are required. Most states require some form of health certificate.

Wherever you go remember that you are responsible for your dog's conduct. The impression you make on hotel and motel managers will determine their attitude toward all dogs and dog-owners. By planning ahead and observing the rules of courtesy, you can take your dog with you anywhere. If your pet enjoys car travel, you, your pet and the entire family can expect a most enjoyable trip.

How to Correct Bad Habits

Puppies learn bad habits rather quickly. As they get older they add to their list. This is partly because of the universal tendency of owners to spoil their pets, and partly because, at the start, the owners think their puppy is being "so cute."

If you start teaching your puppy good habits the day you get him and being stern with him when he starts the bad ones, he'll grow up to be a joy to everyone. Here are some of the common bad habits you can correct.

Garbage Pails — Wastebaskets

No puppy is free of the urge to get into garbage pails and waste-baskets. He's enticed by food odors and by the pleasure of spreading papers and boxes, and tearing them up. The best way to avoid this problem is to place these items in places inaccessible to your dog. If it does occur, scolding will help correct the situation.

Begging

Puppies are inclined to beg when the family is at meals. When he does, scold him and put him into his box bed. He'll learn very quickly that begging doesn't pay. If you give in to him once, you will have corrupted him forever. If you have some tidbits to give him, or a toy bone, don't do so until after the kitchen work has been done.

Jumping On People

It is sort of cute when little puppies climb all over you. But it doesn't stay cute very long. There are three easy ways to cure your puppy. The first consists of gently stepping on his hind toes while he has his front paws on you. The second is to grab his front paws and rush him backward until he falls over back-ward. The third method is to bend your knee and bump him in the chest. In each case, use a stern, firm "No!"

Remember, halfway measures don't work well with puppies. His mother would bite him sharply enough to make him howl if she were training him.

Chewing On Things

All puppies seem to have a destructive urge. Children want to tear things apart "to see what makes them tick." Puppies want to chew things to pieces, partly because dogs are chewing animals and partly out of curiosity. They aren't interested in what you want them to chew on. They'd rather decide for themselves what to tear up.

The universally recommended cure is to give the puppy things he *can* chew on—toys, the specially made rubber bones with built-in smell, actual soupbones—things you have trained him to know are his.

If you catch him in the act, reprimand him immediately, and after a couple of times he will decide it is better not to chew.

Prevention of chewing is sometimes better than the cure. When you have to leave puppy alone for a time, put him into his box bed and give him something he can amuse himself with while you are gone. If you've brought him up to consider the box as his permanent and personal home, he'll remain there happily until you return—and mother's curtains will be safe.

Chasing Cars

We told you in an earlier chapter that dogs which have the age-old patterns of sheep herding in their heredity like to chase running children, bicycles, cars, the milk wagon or anything that moves away from them.

Correction requires the aid of friends. Have someone ride by in a car which has a lot of tantalizing rattles, or have boys ride their bikes by the house while doing a lot of exciting whooping and "hollering."

Puppy is lured into giving chase. Perhaps he thinks he's indulging in some prehistoric wolf chase, or driving cattle, or just joining in the fun. Whichever it is, he's ready for his lesson. As he approaches the slowly moving car or bicycle, you can drown this problem by throwing water on him or using a squirt gun.

Another trick is to have the car or bike stop suddenly with screeching brakes. Whatever method you use, it must be repeated until puppy learns a good habit—not to chase. You may have to repeat this a dozen times in a week. When he'll stand quietly and watch a car or bike go by, praise him for it.

Excessive Barking

Nice dogs can be neighborhood nuisances if they bark too much. You can prevent this by teaching another good habit— not to bark. This is done by setting up conditions under which you know the puppy will bark—arrival of the mailman or milkman, clanking cars going by, or the neighbor's dog.

If the puppy is in the house, scolding and perservance on your part should help. If he is outdoors, turn the hose on him. Always use a stern "No!" as you correct him.

If these "cures" sound severe, remember they may be the difference in having a dog or being forced to dispose of him. You don't want your dog barking at the mailman, since the bark comes before the bite. Neither do you want your dog disturbing the neighbors or chasing children.

Remember also, that you must set up the conditions so that you can repeat the lessons half a dozen times a day until the puppy learns the good habit.

Growling And Biting

Most biting dogs are simply spoiled dogs. They began by growling and got away with that. They then tried snapping and weren't punished for that, and so they made the first bite.

That is a major hurdle. Once a dog has learned he can bite a human being, he no longer can be trusted for he will bite again and again.

Here again, you must set up the conditions. Start by taking puppy's food dish away while he is eating. If he growls, pick him up by the scruff of the neck, so that his front feet are *off* the ground, then slap him gently upward under the chin. Scold him severely, too. Then give him back his food with comforting words and a few pats. Repeat again and again until he knows that he should never growl or bite under any circumstances.

Of course you will romp and play with your puppy. And here again the excitement will make him get too rough. When this happens, you must scold him severely and slap him gently under the chin, while holding his front legs *off* the ground. Having scolded him, make up to him immediately and play with him again. If he starts to get rough, a warning may be enough. Repeat this later in the day, and three or four times in the following days.

In this way, puppy will form the habit of never getting too rough with anyone and of tolerating roughness from small children who do not know they are being rough.

Being A "Bum"

While it is practically impossible to teach a mature dog who is a "bum" to stay in the yard, it is relatively simple to teach a puppy. Here again you are trying to teach a good habit in order that the puppy will not learn a bad one.

The basic problem is to teach the dog the limits of your yard. This done in the following way. Have your puppy on the leash, then start to walk out of your yard. When you reach the edge, you say "No!" and jerk him back. You repeat this several times. Then you get a helper.

The puppy is placed on the training rope and is allowed to

walk along with you. When you reach the edge of the lawn, you say "No!" in a stern voice, and your helper jerks the puppy back. You continue moving out of the yard.

You repeat these two lessons on all sides of the yard until puppy gets the idea. Next, you have some one call puppy or you lure him with another dog he'd like to see. Each time, he is jerked back at the edge of the yard. Or have the person who called the dog punish him if he leaves the yard.

In this way, the puppy learns the limits of the yard and never to leave it. But you must take one further step until the puppy is old enough to know the difference. It is this: Do not take the puppy from the yard unless in a car. In this way, you won't confuse him. As he grows older, he'll understand the difference.

The Mailman

As a proud dog owner you will be ashamed to know that a hundred thousand dogs bite mailmen, deliverymen, meter readers or garbage collectors each year. This is partly the fault of the people bitten, for they do not take the time to get acquainted with the dogs and to assure them that they are on the grounds for a good reason. But it is partly the dog owner's fault, too, because he hasn't taught his dog to understand.

Since excessive barking almost always leads to biting unless prevented, you should introduce your dog to mail, delivery, and garbage men.

Take the dog up to these people, use encouraging words and urge the dog to be friends, assuring him that nothing is wrong. Have the stranger pet the dog, too. Finally, tell all regular delivery people the name of your dog.

A Visit To The Veterinarian? *Keep your dog on a leash!*

When visiting the veterinary hospital, be sure and keep the dog on a leash or under your control at all times. Nothing is more exasperating to all concerned than a dog running loose in the waiting room. Fights often result between unrestrained dogs. Irresponsible pet owners frequently let their dogs urinate on planters, walls, chairs, etc.

Be courteous and considerate by keeping your dog on a leash, holding onto his collar or sitting in your lap.

Simple Obedience Training

Obedience and trick training mean, for the dog, learning a new language. Use simple commands of one word each where possible, such as "Heel" and "Sit." This will make it easy for the dog to associate the command with the lesson he is learning.

Meanwhile, experiment with your own voice. Your commands should be stern and convincing, but don't shout so loud as to blow down the building. Similarly, when you praise your dog, put praise into your voice. In this case, say "Good dog," and put praise into your petting, too. Make your lessons not more than 10 minutes at a time.

All training begins with the dog sitting at your left heel. You can't teach a dog anything if he is galloping away. Neither can you teach him if he is wandering mentally. You must have his attention.

If you are starting with a small puppy, you can teach him to wait in a corner until you have put his supper on the floor and have given him the signal to eat. Some people think of this as a trick. But actually it is one of the basic lessons in dog training—to sit and stay until told he can get up.

Here are some of the more important lessons which are basic for all training, including field work. You will need a good leather leash, a strong collar (preferably a chain training collar) and a lot of patience.

"Sit"

In a commanding voice, tell your dog to "Sit." At the same instant, pull back on his collar and push down on his rump. It may be necessary for you to wiggle his rump in order to get

off balance so that he has to sit. Hold him in position, repeating the command word "Sit." Then praise him, saying "Good dog."

Move along a bit, then repeat the lesson. Do this over and over until the dog will sit on command.

"Heel"

The purpose of this exercise is to teach the dog to walk quietly at your left side. Hold the end of the leash in your right hand and use your left to hold the leash fairly close to the dog's neck.

Command him in a firm voice to "Heel" and start walking forward. If the dog pulls ahead, use a wrist action to give a series of quick jerks to bring him back to heel. If he lags behind, the same short jerks will bring him forward. But you must keep repeating the command "Heel" until he learns that it means he must walk at your side.

This lesson is more easily taught if you do it along a quiet street, a sidewalk or building. The idea is to give the dog knowledge of the *exact distance* he should keep from your heel. Thus, if you walk forward along the left curb of a street, the dog must stay close to your side. If he jumps off the curb, say "No!" and jerk him back. Walking along the sidewalk edge

also helps. If the dog is between you and a building, you can space him perfectly, moving closer to head him off if he tries to get ahead.

Dogs that pull wildly on the leash, choke, and lunge require patience and firmness and perhaps special collars, but must be corrected. You might use a cane to tap the dog lightly on the nose when he gets too far ahead, or swing the cane in an arc so that, if he goes forward, the cane will bump him in the nose or face.

You can combine the "Sit" and "Heel" lessons, as your dog will learn both of them as easily as he'll learn one alone. Walk the dog at heel, then stop and, at the same instant, command and force the dog to sit. After a time, the dog learns to walk quietly at heel and to sit when you stop. Give him a lot of petting and compliments during this training.

You can teach your dog heeling and sitting, on leash, in three or four days. But the test comes when other dogs are near. When your dog will pay attention to you and mind in the presence of other dogs, you've won the major battle.

Do not practice these lessons more than 10 minutes at a time or the dog will get bored. After a few minutes of practice give him a play period, then give him another period of training.

Heeling Off The Leash

Next, teach your dog to obey even when not on leash. Give him five minutes' work on the leash. Then take his leash off while he is sitting. Use your most threatening voice, command "Heel!" and start walking. Be ready to grab him if he gives any indication of "taking off." Also, you can use the palm of your left hand to guide him so that he doesn't get ahead of you.

If he does get away from you, catch him but don't scold him. Immediately put him back on the leash for a little more work. When he responds, try him off the leash again. Obviously, it's best to practice this in a closed yard.

Your dog is not well trained until he will walk quietly at heel, sitting when you stop, starting when you start, without a command.

Because they give you their attention, most hunting dogs will learn to heel and sit, on and off a leash, in two weeks, depending a little on your own ability as a trainer. Terriers, because of their "devil take it" attitude, may require longer periods of training.

Come When Called

This is the most important and perhaps the most difficult lesson to teach. The reason is, if a dog gets beyond your control and won't listen to you, he'll take advantage of you. Moreover, he understands this quickly and takes full advantage of the situation.

For this lesson you'll need a length of Venetian-blind cord 40 to 50 feet long. Stretch this to get the kinks out, then tie one end to the dog's collar. Allow him to drag the rope about until he's used to it. You should *wear gloves* to prevent painful rope burns.

When puppy is going the other way, call him by name. Then begin to pull him in to you. He may resist a bit, but keep pulling and calling him at the same time. When you have him in front of you, make him sit, them compliment and pet him.

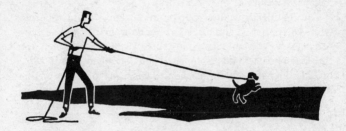

Repeat this lesson again and again, all the time inventing conditions under which he'll think he can disobey. For instance, put his food dish in the kitchen, take the cord into the living room, and then call and pull him to you. After petting, send him back to the kitchen to his food.

Put his food dish around the corner of the house so that he thinks you can't see him. Call him and begin pulling. Take him for long walks and when he starts to gallop off to visit another dog, call him and begin to haul him in.

When your dog will come instantly, while on the rope and with no pulling, try him when he is free of it. It is best to do this in a small, enclosed area so that if he disobeys you can chase him down quickly and return him to the spot from which you called. Then try him in a bigger area.

Of course, you must practice with him in the presence of other dogs. If you live in the city you may want to teach him to come on a "silent" whistle. The procedure is the same. Instead of calling him by voice give a series of short, quick blasts on the whistle. The "silent" whistle vibrations are above those which the human ear can receive but the dog can hear them very well.

In training, your dog sometimes may get six to a dozen feet from you, then keep just that distance away. All animals instinctively know the safe distance to place between themselves and an enemy. The dog uses this to keep you from catching him.

A simple way to bridge this gap is to throw something in back of him. Almost invariably it will startle him and cause him to rush to your heel. When he does, compliment and pet him.

"Sit" And "Stay"

If you practiced making your puppy sit and stay in a corner while you prepared and placed his food on the floor, this lesson will be easy. You can teach it also at any stage of training. Stop the dog at heel and make him sit. Then command "Stay," while placing the palm of your left hand against his face. Keep commanding "Stay" and slowly walk around him. If he gets up, force him back into sit position at the exact spot from which he got up.

When you can walk around your dog without movement on his part, give him the stay command and step right in front of him. Restrain him with the palm of your hand, and then slowly back away.

Keep commanding him to stay, and keep your palm out in front of you as a warning. If he gets up, say "No!" and rush to him, lift him by the scruff of the neck, and take him back to the spot from which he left.

When he will stay in position, try turning your back to him. If he'll stay, walk away a few yards, then return to heel. Compliment and pet him. Now command him sternly to stay, using the palm of your hand, turned backward this time, as a warning, and walk slowly forward. Go about 30 feet, turn and face the dog for a few moments, then return to the heel position.

Your next lesson is to place him at sit position, command him to stay, then walk out of sight. Go into a building or around a corner. Walk into some place where you can observe him through a window. If he gets up, rush to him and replace him. At first, you should be out of sight only a few seconds. Gradually increase the time to three or four minutes.

The last step in this lesson is to make him sit and stay in the presence of other dogs. You can do this by having neighbors bring their dogs during the training lesson.

"Lie Down"

While we have titled this "Lie Down," the proper command is simply "Down," given in as commanding a voice as possible. You can teach this in one of several ways. One is, with the dog sitting, to give the command, then shove down on his shoulders, at the same time wobbling him off balance. This works with most dogs.

The second method is to place the leash between the sole and heel of your shoe. Give the command "Down," then pull up on the leash. This pulls his neck down and forces him to go down. When you see that he is starting to go down, compliment him. Also, you can pull his legs forward until he is down.

With many dogs, you have to teach the difference between "Sit" and "Down." If the dog goes down on the sit command, say "No!" and lift him into sitting position, while giving the command to "Sit." Likewise, if he starts to sit or stand when you've put him down you must immediately reprove him and put him back in the down position.

"Down" and "Stay"

The purpose is to keep the dog at stay position when lying down. This is not difficult if you already have taught your dog the sit and stay positions and if he obeys the command "Down." Start with the down position, then teach the dog to remain in that position while you walk around him, over him, and walk out of sight. If the dog starts to get up, say "No!" and see that he returns to the down position. You must see that he stays down until he is told to sit. Remember that you should not tell him to sit until you have returned to the position that places him at your left heel.

In all of these lessons try to vary conditions so that your dog learns always to obey. Varying the procedure will keep him interested in his work. For instance, try training him in a field, in swampy area, and near a stream. The enticing smells will distract his attention and he'll want to disobey or will forget to obey. Each lesson under these differing conditions will be worth two under the same old conditions. They will improve your dog's training and make you a proud owner.

To say "Well, he does this perfectly at home" is a lame excuse, almost worse than none.

It is possible that you can find an obedience training class near you. You should look for one, since group training is the best possible experience for your dog. Also, the trainer of such a class may be able to help you correct any faults in your home training.

Summary

Use a stern and commanding, but not loud, voice. Use one-word commands where possible. Dogs get bored and tired, so work only 10 minutes at a time.

All training starts with the dog sitting at heel, but you can teach "Heel" and "Sit" at the same time. Remember that your dog must obey. Don't let him get away with anything. Use plenty of praise and petting when the dog performs correctly.

Write the Purina Dog Care Center for these Booklets

■ **How to Understand and Enjoy a Dog Show—No. GP 6092.** Basic training in the rules, regulations and running of a dog show.

■ **How to Understand and Enjoy An Obedience Trial—No. GP 6293.** Complete background and things to look for when watching an obedience trial.

■ **On Being a Good Pet Neighbor—No. GP 5265.** A frank discussion of your responsibilities (moral and legal) as a pet owner.

To order these free booklets, or to obtain specific information on the care of dogs, write:

Purina Dog Care Center
Checkerboard Square
St. Louis, Mo. 63188

**For Your Cat
Purina's
"Handbook of Cat Care"**

17 fact-filled illustrated chapters.
Send 25¢ to cover postage and handling to:

> Handbook of Cat Care
> P.O. Box 9092
> St. Paul, Minn. 55190

Some Tricks to Teach Your Dog

Once you've taught your puppy or grown dog basic obedience, it is comparatively simple to teach him tricks. There are two reasons for this: You've taught the dog to give you its full attention, and you've placed it under your control.

Puppies learn more quickly than older dogs. But the saying "You can't teach an old dog new tricks" really refers to humans and not dogs. If you can get and hold your dog's attention, you can teach him many tricks. In basic obedience, you've already taught your dog to sit and to lie down. So let's go on from there.

"Sit Up"

Have your dog sit in a corner, as close to the walls as he can. This will prevent him from falling over backward. Now gently lift his front legs while commanding him to "Sit up." He will want to stand on his hind legs so it will be necessary to shove him into the sitting-up position. Repeat this several times until

you are certain he has the idea and will sit up. Then take your hands off him and give the command. If he does not obey, help him up again. Sometimes you can tantalize him into sitting up by dangling a bit of dog food above his nose. This should be used only as a last resort, since you don't want him to get the idea that he needn't sit up unless you have the reward handy. Also, the reward takes his mind off the training.

When the dog will sit up in the corner, try him in other places. Each time he does sit up, make him stay there by warning commands, then say "All right" or "Okay" to let him know the lesson is over. Then pet him a lot.

"Play Catch"

Have the dog sit in a corner in a well-lighted room. Get some small pieces of dog food. When you are sure you have his attention, toss the food at his face and say "Catch." He won't budge and the food will fall to the floor. Now you must rush forward and grab it before he does. Replace him in position and tell him to stay. Be sure he is watching your hand, toss the food, and repeat the command "Catch."

You may have to repeat this half a dozen times. Eventually he'll realize he must catch the food in the air. When he does, compliment him and repeat the exercise. Since he eats each bit of food you throw to him you can repeat this many times without boring him.

You can, if you like, try the same thing with a small ball. Place him in the corner before you throw the ball. Otherwise he may try to run off with it. At this stage you only want him to play catch. Retrieving it is a different lesson.

To "Carry"

Properly taught, dogs take great pride in carrying things for their owners. It fulfills their ancient desire of 20,000 years ago to co-operate with man. Set the dog in the corner. Roll a newspaper and fasten it with a rubber band or string. Kneel beside the dog. Put your left hand over his jaw, command him to "Carry," and then force open his mouth by pressing his lips against the teeth. When you have his mouth open, put in the newspaper.

He'll try to spit it out. But hold it in his mouth, repeating sternly, "Carry." Then say "Okay" or "All right" to let him know that the lesson is over. Then pet him a lot. Repeat this until he will open his mouth and take the newspaper on command. This is an unpleasant exercise for him at first so don't overdo it in the beginning.

When the dog will hold the paper until you tell him he can release it, you are ready for the next step. Put him in the corner and fasten his leash to his collar. Command him to carry, then begin to walk him gently forward. If he tries to drop the newspaper use your most commanding voice, and, at the same time, use your right hand to force him to hold the paper. Give him plenty of petting and compliments for this when he does it right.

It will require only a lesson or two to give him the idea to carry. After that let him walk at heel and compliment him as he carries. You'll see how proud he'll be. When he has demonstrated great pride in carrying, begin making him carry other things.

Never at any time during these lessons allow him to drop the article before you tell him he can. He must always give it directly into your hand. If you allow him to get away with dropping it even once, you'll never be able to depend upon him.

"Fetch"

Practically any dog will chase a ball. And sometimes, almost any dog will bring it back. The well-trained dog will chase any thrown object and bring it back directly to your hand. He should, moreover, sit down in front of you before delivering it to your hand.

If you've taught your dog to carry properly, the next step is fairly simple. Put him in the corner, kneel beside him, show him the object, but don't give it to him. Instead, throw it a few feet. Command "Fetch." If he doesn't move, lead him to the object, draw his head down to it, force him to open his mouth and then "cheat a little" by lifting the object to help it into his mouth. Command him again to "Fetch" and make him carry the object back to his corner.

Once he's got the idea, he'll chase and fetch with as much pride as he carries. But again, use plenty of petting and complimenting while you are teaching him.

You can vary the "Fetch" procedure by teaching your dog to find and fetch. For example, by repeating the word "dish" and giving him his dish to carry, he'll learn what that word means. Gradually you can teach him to go into another room to find and fetch his dish. Eventually you'll be able to send him for slippers and several other articles. Once the dog has learned to find and fetch he takes such pleasure in it that he'll beg you to hide things for him.

"Roll Over"

Command your dog to roll over. Do this while he's lying down. He won't understand, so make rolling over motions with your hands. Do this three or four times, repeating the command "Roll over," then grab his legs and roll him over. Praise him even though you forcibly rolled him over. Sometimes it helps if you yourself roll over.

"Jump"

Put your dog on a leash, have him walk at heel and then walk toward some low object. Jump over, yourself, and jerk the dog slightly so that he jumps, too.

Command "Jump" each time. Repeat this over and over, choosing higher things until the dog has to make a considerable jump. Next, lead him toward the object to be jumped, but you pass to the right of it so that only the dog has to do the jumping. Now, make the dog sit on one side of the hurdle, give the "Stay" command, and you go to the other. Tug slightly up on the leash, command "Jump" and make the dog jump toward you. After he has learned to jump over *with* you and *toward* you when you are on the other side, both on and off the leash, then place him in front of the hurdle and you stand at the *side*. Command him to jump. If he does not, go to him and make him. If he starts to go around instead of jumping the hurdle, scold him and make him jump as ordered. You'll have to repeat this only a couple of times before he'll jump on command from any position.

You can have fun by teaching him to jump over a friend who is kneeling on the ground and even over two or three friends. Eventually you may be able to make him jump over a friend's dog.

"Dont Touch It"

This lesson is something more than a trick. You should teach your dog not to touch food offered it by a stranger. You start by putting the leash on the dog. You let him approach a piece of food on the floor. Then just as he reaches for it, say "No" and jerk him back. Your dog should already understand the meaning of "No" very well. He'll get the idea quickly that he can't touch anything you've ordered him not to touch.

Next, have your friends offer him food. Again you jerk him back and command "No." Occasionally give him a bit of food as a reward. But keep repeating the lesson until he automatically will draw back from anything a stranger offers him.

Summary

Dogs love to do tricks but—as in basic obedience—trick training requires that the dog learn he must obey your command. Keep your lessons short—not over five or ten minutes at a time for a single trick. After working on one trick, let your dog have recreation by performing another trick. This will make him proud and happy. When your dog learns one trick it makes him ready to learn another. As he gets the idea, there is almost no limit to the number you can teach him.

REGULAR FLAVOR
PURINA DOG CHOW…
available in 2 lb., 5 lb.,
10 lb., 25 lb., and 50 lb.
bags.

BEEF-BACON &
CHEESE FLAVOR DOG
CHOW…available in
5 lb., 10 lb., and 25 lb.
bags.

LIVER FLAVOR
PURINA DOG CHOW…
available in 5 lb., 10 lb.,
25 lb., and 50 lb. bags.

BEEF & EGG FLAVOR
PURINA DOG CHOW…
available in 5 lb., 10 lb.,
and 25 lb. bags.

COMPLETE FOOD FOR
DOGS…available in 2
lb., 5 lb., 10 lb., 25 lb.
and 40 lb. bags.

THE HIGH PROTEIN
DOG MEAL for active
dogs…available in
5 lb., 10 lb., 25 lb., and
50 lb. bags.

THE SPECIAL FORMULA PUPPY FOODS…available in 2 lb.,
5 lb., 10 lb., 25 lb., and 40 lb. bags. Regular and Beef Flavor
Puppy Chow.

Dog Breeds of the World

Genetically speaking, the dog is not highly developed. Scientists say it has a "plastic germ plasm." This means its type is easily changed by selective breeding. It is estimated that there are more than 400 dog breeds in the world. In contrast, there are only 36 cat breeds, wild and domestic.

When primitive men wandered the world, they took their dogs with them. They were forced to do so by the Ice Ages, population pressures, famines, and other factors. Their dogs probably mated with primitive and differently developing cousins.

Barriers of ice, mountains, and oceans separated tribes of people and their dogs. Environmental factors and the barriers of geography and climate caused a certain amount of inbreeding. And thus distinct races of both humans and dogs developed. They differed physically but not very much mentally. They were still all human and all dog.

Shepherd people the world over have developed herding dogs. These might differ radically, except for their herding aptitudes and their weather-resistant coats. Most have long coats, with soft, dense, water-proof undercoats. Some have flat coats, with less undercoat.

Great civilizations have tended to develop types of dogs. Thus, the Egyptians and neighboring empires developed the Greyhound type, as represented by that breed, the Saluki, Afghan, and others. By 400 B. C., the Greeks had developed trailing breeds or hounds. During the Middle Ages, terriers were developed. The word comes from the Latin "terra," meaning earth. Terriers went into the burrows or dens of foxes and other animals after the hounds had brought the quarry to bay.

But the rise of type, as the modern world knows it, began with the introduction of dog shows. The first dog show was held in England in 1859. American dog shows began about 1870. Many breeds became "fixed" shortly after 1900. Thus, only a very few breeds can be called ancient, but all are examples of man-made development or evolution.

Today, the American Kennel Club recognizes more than 120 breeds, and, in addition, some are split into varieties. Others do not have full stud book status, but can be shown in miscellaneous classes. Most, but not all, of the Canadian breed standards correspond with those adopted by the A.K.C.

It may be well to make some general and interesting points about the dog breeds, their origin, and the pronunciation of their names. This will, of course, include some "don'ts."

The name Affenpinscher may give you trouble. It is a combination of two words which mean "monkey terrier."

The Pomeranian was once a sled dog and has been bred down to his present size in about 100 years. You'll note how spunky he is. He still hasn't discovered he's now a toy dog.

The Chihuahua is named after the Mexican state of that name, though the true origin of the breed is unknown. He is, on the average, the smallest breed in the world.

The Brittany Spaniel is the world's only pointing spaniel.

The Miniature Pinscher is not a Miniature Doberman. The breed is very old, whereas the Doberman was developed by Louis Doberman of Apolda, Germany, about 1890.

The Poodle was once a sporting dog, and his name was "wasserhund" or water dog. Do not call him a French Poodle, though he might be one if he came from France. Call him simply a Poodle, or use his correct variety name—Standard, Miniature, or Toy.

Don't call a Boston Terrier a Boston Bull, Boston Bull Terrier, or Toy Bulldog. Boston Terrier is his correct name. The Bulldog comes from England, but his name is simply Bulldog. The French Bulldog comes from France, and that's his correct name.

There are two Manchester Terriers, the Standard and the Toy. Don't call them "rat terriers" or "black and tan terriers." Do not call the Shetland Sheepdog a "Toy Collie," nor the German Shepherd a "German Police Dog." Correct pronunciation for Dachshund is "docks-hund," and for Samoyed is "Sam-o-yed."

Registered Breeds

Here are the breeds eligible for registry in the stud book of the American Kennel Club, and which therefore can compete in field trials, bench shows, and obedience trials held under American Kennel Club license.

In addition to the above breeds, the American Kennel Club places 6 more breeds in the Miscellaneous Class. These are rare breeds, and there are insufficient numbers of them to merit opening the stud book to them. However, they may be shown in the Miscellaneous Class at dog shows.

There are other stud books besides that of the American Kennel Club. But it is the most important in the Western Hemisphere. Its system of classifying dogs into six groups is followed in Canada, Mexico and all of South America.

 Sporting Dogs

American Water Spaniels
Brittany Spaniels
Chesapeake Bay Retrievers
Clumber Spaniels
Cocker Spaniels
Curly-Coated Retrievers
English Cocker Spaniels
English Setters
English Springer Spaniels
Field Spaniels
Flat-Coated Retrievers
German Short-haired Pointers
German Wire-haired Pointers
Golden Retrievers
Gordon Setters
Irish Setters
Irish Water Spaniels
Labrador Retrievers
Pointers
Sussex Spaniels
Vizslas
Weimaraners
Welsh Springer Spaniels
Wirehaired Pointing Griffons

 Hound Breeds

Afghans
Basenjis
Basset Hounds
Beagles
Black and Tan Coonhounds
Bloodhounds
Borzois
Dachshunds
Scottish Deerhounds
American Foxhounds
English Foxhounds
Greyhounds
Harriers
Ibizan Hounds
Norwegian Elkhounds
Otter Hounds
Rhodesian Ridgebacks
Salukis
Whippets
Irish Wolfhounds

Working Dogs

Akitas
Alaskan Malamutes
Bearded Collies
Belgian Malinois
Belgian Sheepdogs
Belgian Tervuren
Bernese Mountain Dogs
Bouvier Des Flandres
Boxers
Briards
Bullmastiffs
Collies
Doberman Pinschers
German Shepherds
Great Danes
Great Pyrenees
Komondor
Kuvasz
Mastiffs
Newfoundlands
Old English Sheepdogs
Pulik
Rottweilers
Samoyeds
Giant Schnauzers
Standard Schnauzers
Shetland Sheepdogs
Siberian Huskies
St. Bernards
Cardigan Welsh Corgis
Pembroke Welsh Corgis

Terriers

Airedale Terriers
American
   Staffordshire
   Terriers
Australian Terriers
Bedlington Terriers
Border Terriers
Bull Terriers
Cairn Terriers
Dandie Dinmont
   Terriers
Fox Terriers
   (Wire & Smooth)
Irish Terriers
Kerry Blue Terriers
Lakeland Terriers
Manchester Terriers
   (Standard & Toy)
Norfolk Terriers
Norwich Terriers
Miniature
   Schnauzers
Scotish Terriers
Sealyham Terriers
Skye Terriers
Soft-Coated
   Wheaten
   Terriers
Staffordshire Bull
   Terriers
Welsh Terriers
West Highland
   White Terriers

Non-Sporting Dogs

Bichon Frises
Boston Terriers
Bulldogs
Chow Chows
Dalmatians
French Bulldogs
Keeshonden
Lhasa Apsos
Poodles (Standard,
   Miniature, Toy)
Schipperkes
Tibetan Terriers

Toy Dogs

Affenpinschers	Maltese	Pomeranians
Chihuahuas	Papillons	Pugs
English Toy Spaniels	Pekingese	Shih Tzu
Brussels Griffons	Miniature Pinschers	Silky Terriers
Italian Greyhounds		Yorkshire Terriers
Japanese Chin		

Miscellaneous Category
(AKC recognized but not
registrable; eligible for
most obedience trials)

Australian Cattle Dog
Australian Kelpie

Border Collies
Cavalier King
   Charles Spaniel
Miniature Bull Terrier
Spinoni Italiani

The United Kennel Club is another registry for dogs which
compete in UKC field trials, foxhound trials, night hunts and
water races around the United States.

Breeds Registered by the UKC

**The United Kennel Club
321 West Cedar Street
Kalamazoo, Mi. 49006**

American (Pit) Bull Terrier	Boxer	Fox Terrier, Smooth
American Toy Terrier	Miniature Boxer	Fox Terrier, Wire
	Chihuahua	Fox Terrier, Toy
American Eskimo	Chow Chow	German Shepherd
American Water Spaniel	Collie	Great Dane
	Collie Columbian	Greyhound
Alaskan Malamute	Collie, Smooth	Pekingese
Airedale Terrier	Dachshund, Smooth	Pomeranian
Arctic Huskie	Dachshund, Longhaired	Poodle
Basset Hound		St. Bernard
Beagle	Dalmatian	Scottish Terrier
Bloodhound	English Shepherd	Spaniel, Cocker
Boston Terrier		Whippet

 **Coonhound Breeds**

American Black & Tan Coonhound	English Coonhound
American Black & Tan Fox & Coonhound	Plott Hound
Bluetick Coonhound	Redbone Coonhound
	Walker (Treeing Coonhound)

Summary

The dog has a "plastic germ plasm" which permits almost limitless variations in type. Man's wanderings, plus barriers of ice, mountains, and oceans, helped to develop type. The Civilizations of Asia Minor developed coursing or "chasing" dogs, while the tracking and bird dogs were developed by Europeans. The "don'ts" in dogdom include the mispronunication of breed names. The American Kennel Club system of classifying breeds is followed in the entire Western Hemisphere.

Reference Books:

Dogs Of The World, by Dr. Erich Schneider-Leyer; Popular Dogs, London, publishers.

The Complete Dog Book, published by the American Kennel Club, 51 Madison Avenue, New York, New York 10010. Contains the histories and standards of all the recognized breeds, and a veterinary section.

The Modern Dog Encyclopedia, edited by Henry P. Davis; Stackpole and Heck, publishers.

The Observer's Book Of Dogs, by Clifford Hubbard; Frederick Warne & Co., New York, distributors. An English book which gives short descriptions of more than 200 breeds of dogs.

The Natural History Of Dogs, by Richard and Alice Fiennes published by Bonanza Books of Crown Publishers, New York.

American Kennel Club
51 Madison Avenue
New York, NY 10010

Sporting Dogs

Pointer

There are three basic types of sporting dogs, divided according to their use. These are the pointing breeds, the spaniel or flushing breeds, and those used primarily for retrieving, often in the water. There are exceptions. For instance, the Brittany Spaniel is the world's only pointing spaniel. Irish and American Water Spaniels are used chiefly as retrievers.

The pointing breeds, with the exception noted, correspond in many respects. They will weigh 50 to 85 pounds. They are approximately square in body, being as long as tall, measuring from the ground to the top of the shoulder, and from there to the root of the tail. All are primarily bird hunters.

Best known is the Pointer. But we have also the German Shorthaired Pointer and the Weimaraner. The Pointer's tail should reach only to the hock joint; the other two have docked tails. All are short-coated.

English Setter

The English, Irish and Gordon Setters are long-coated dogs and have long tails. English Setter colors are usually black and white, orange or blue belton. Irish Setters are dark red; Gordons are black and tan.

Best known of the flushing spaniels are the American Cocker, English Cocker and English Springer. American Cockers have somewhat shorter muzzles than do English Cockers and Springers. Originally any spaniel under 28 pounds

Cocker Spaniel

was a Cocker (used on woodcock) and any over 28 was a Springer.

American Cockers should be 15½ inches or under at the shoulder; English Cockers are slightly taller. English Springers are about 20 inches. All three should have dense, flat or wavy coats. The ear leather should reach the nose and the ear is set level with the eye or lower. The top line slopes slightly from the withers to root of the tail. The tail is docked (to save damage in briar patches).

Labrador Retriever

The retrievers, too, are roughly square in body. The Labradors are usually black or yellow. They have heavy tails, particularly at the base, and are often rather heavy-headed. They are 22 to 25 inches at the shoulder.

Golden Retrievers are a rich golden color but with a range to cream. Their height and weight are about the same as the Labrador but they are less barrelchested and they have long coats. Chesapeake Bays have wavy, dead-grass-colored coats. They are higher in the hips than the other retrievers and may sag a bit in the back.

The Irish and American Water Spaniels are liver-colored with the former being about average size for a sporting dog and the latter slightly more than half that large. They have thick curly coats but with only lightly covered tails—rat tails, as some call them.

Hound Breeds

Beagle

The Hound Group is made up of two very different types of hound—the scent follower and the sight hunter or "sight hound."

The Beagle is the best-known scent-follower tracking dog in America since he is the country's most popular hound breed. He comes in two sizes—13 inches or under and over 13 inches but not over 15 inches. He is a carbon copy of the larger Harrier and the still larger English Foxhound.

Hounds in this family are usually black, tan, and white. But a good hound can be any color. Their coat is short and glossy. The tail is carried gaily but not squirrel fashion. The ears are set at eye level, drop beside cheeks, and have fine leather.

Dachshund

Dachshunds and Bassets are similar in body but the latter has a sort of Bloodhound head on a Dachshund body. The Dachshund is one of the world's most popular breeds.

The Dachshund has a wedge-shaped head, ears set low with fine leather, a sloping shoulder covering an immense chest, a level back, and tail which is not carried too gaily. He is low to the ground, designed to go into rabbit holes or other similar lairs. Dachshunds are usually red or dark brown or black and tan. They come in smooth, long or wire-haired coats.

Basset

The Basset is twice as large as the biggest Dachshunds. His ears are almost long enough to wrap around his head. His skin is loose and elastic. Bassets are usually black, tan, and white.

In the sight-hunter group are the Greyhounds, Wolfhounds, and Whippets. These dogs are so made that they run in huge leaps, driving their hind legs ahead of their front ones. Because of the back and leg structure they are often called "wheeled back" hounds.

These breeds are all streamlined. Their muzzles are wedge-shaped; the ears "button back" against the neck; heart and lung room is obtained by the great depth of chest and narrowness rather than barrel in the ribs. The tail is long and is used as a rudder to help maintain balance when at full speed.

Greyhound

Because they are used at dog tracks for racing and on the western plains for coursing, Greyhounds are the most popular. Whippets are smaller editions of Greyhounds. They do not chase the artificial rabbit but run 200-yard dash courses.

Afghans and Borzois (Russian Wolfhounds) are densely coated. The former resembles the Saluki but has a longer and denser coat. The Borzoi and Irish Wolfhound are among the tallest of the dog breeds with some reaching 32 inches or more at the shoulder.

Working Dogs

Boxer

As the term suggests, the dogs which make up this group were developed to labor for a living. They might pull milk carts, do police duty, carry messages, or guard and herd sheep, cattle or other animals.

Starting about 1934, the Boxer began to become a world-wide favorite. He once was shown in the nonsporting group as a sort of Bulldog. His muzzle does give that impression. He is undershot, has a short, broad muzzle with nose pushed slightly back. His ears are usually cropped and thus stand erect.

Boxers measure 22 to 24 inches tall. They are fawn and brindle, with white markings on the face, feet and chest. A black mask is required and the dog should not have more than one-third of its body colored white.

German Shepherd

The German Shepherd is also a world-wide favorite. He is longer than tall, his ears stand erect without cropping and he has a dense, double, but usually flat, coat. His top line slopes from withers to hips. He has very strongly angulated hind quarters and a long, bushy tail.

German Shepherds weigh 75 to 85 pounds, occasionally more. Their colors are jet black to light gray and can be black and tan, brindle, iron gray, and gray with sable markings.

Collie

The Collie has always ranked high in popularity. In recent years the Shetland Sheepdog has come to look like the Collie. The "Sheltie" is 13 to 16 inches at the shoulder, the Collie, 24 inches. Both have very heavy weather-resistant coats with so dense an undercoat that it is difficult to find the skin.

These two are the only shepherd breeds in which the eyes are not set forward. With these two the muzzle line obstructs the view so that each eye sees only on that side.

Colors are sable and white, black, tan and white, and blue merle and white (in the Collie). When the merle colors appear, it is common to see the blue, wall or china eye. The ears are carried erect and should "break" and tip forward.

Doberman Pinscher

Louis Doberman of Apolda, Germany, began trying to breed a giant terrier about 1875. He wanted a guard and working dog with the agility of the terrier. He used Rottweiler, Greyhound and Manchester Terrier blood. The breed began to appear in its present shape after 1890.

The Doberman stands 25 inches tall. He has a long wedge-shaped muzzle with ears cropped and erect. He is square in body and his tail is docked at the body. The top line slopes from withers to root of tail. The coat is smooth and short. Colors are black and tan, red, and blue.

85

Terriers

Wirehair Fox Terrier

In this group of dogs are generally those which go into the earth, "terra," after game. Their job was to go into holes that were too small for the larger hounds and there do battle with and bring out or kill the quarry. For centuries farmers have used them to keep down rats and vermin. Big-game hunters have relied on the larger terrier breeds to go in and finish off the quarry in close fighting. Their courage, ability and style have always won the admiration of dog lovers everywhere.

Terriers can generally be divided into two groups—the short-legged small breeds and the longer-legged, larger dogs. Better known in the former class are the Cairn, Dandie Dinmont, Scottish, Sealyham and West Highland White Terriers. In the second group are the Airedale, Bedlington, Bull Terriers, Irish, Fox Terriers (wire and smooth), Kerry Blue and Welsh Terriers, and the Miniature Schnauzer, relative newcomer to the Terrier group. All are popular as pets and show dogs.

Schnauzer

The Fox Terrier has remained a popular favorite for many years. Small and compact of body, he can take a lot of rough-and-tumble play without much damage to himself. The Wire and the Smooth are but two varieties of the same breed and the same standard applies to both. They should not exceed 15½ " in height at the shoulders and should weigh about 18 pounds. Their color is predominantly white with black and tan markings.

The Miniature Schnauzer, gaining in popularity among the terriers, is a pepper-and-salt color, including red pepper, and black. His ears are cropped and stand erect. The tail is cut to three joints and stands erect. He is about 12½ inches tall.

The Cairn, Scottish Terrier, Sealyham and West Highland White are supposed to have short bodies. And they do, but their legs are shorter still. A West Highland White is not to be confused with a white Scottie, which it closely resembles.

Scottish Terrier

Scottish Terriers stand about 10 inches at the shoulder and have tails seven inches long. They have stout bodies—well let down between the ribs—and have a fairly level top line. Their coats are harsh and wiry and about two inches long. Colors are iron gray, black, sandy or even wheaten.

Airedale

The Airedale is the world's largest terrier, standing 23 inches at the shoulder and weighing about 40 pounds. Skull and muzzle are about the same length. The ears hang to the side instead of falling forward as they do on the Fox and Irish. Color is tan with blankets of black or red brindle. The Kerry Blue Terrier is slightly smaller in size but has the same general shape. His color is dark blue-black or steel gray.

Toy Dogs

Chihuahua

The toy breeds can be described as those dogs weighing between 1½ and 18 pounds. Some Chihuahuas are as small as the former, and the latter is the top weight for the Pug. Because of their small size, the toy breeds are very popular as house pets and companions. They are very alert and make excellent watchdogs.

The Chihuahua (pronounced "Shee-wah-wah") is high in numbers registered. There are two varieties, smooth- and long-coated. Present-day Chihuahuas have achieved nearly sporting-dog soundness of legs and feet. They are slightly longer than tall, however. The ears flare to the sides when not at attention but are fairly erect otherwise. The tail can curve over the back, be carried gaily or even horizontally. Chihuahua breeders usually want females larger than males since females under three pounds do not produce well as brood matrons.

Pekingese

The Pekingese is another of the world's most popular breeds, and this despite small litters and serious whelping problems. It has enormous eyes. You should be able to place a ruler so that the tip of the forehead, nose and lower jaw touch the ruler to form a line about 15 degrees from perpendicular. The nose should touch a horizontal line just above the midpoint of the eyes.

The "Peke" is the only dog whose standard calls for flat feet. He has heart-shaped ears, should have a reasonably level back, and has a great plume of a tail which often touches his head when brushed over his back. They must weigh under 14 pounds.

Pomeranian

We have told you elsewhere that the Pomeranian was once a sled dog. He comes from the same family as the Spitz and the Keeshond. Poms have foxy expressions, caused by short, pointed muzzles and triangular ears which, though not small, are nearly hidden in their thick hair. They have a stand-off coat and come in a variety of colors. Most modern Pomeranians weigh seven pounds or less.

Pug

The Pug looks something like a Pekingese would if totally clipped. His outstanding features are a massive round skull, heavy skull wrinkles, a short, level back and a tail which curls over the back. A double curl is ideal. Pugs weigh 14 to 18 pounds. In silvers, apricots and fawns, a trace of black should run along the top of the back from the occiput to the tail. Nails should be black. Some Pugs are solid black in color.

Other popular members of the toy group are Miniature Pinschers, Toy Manchesters and Poodles, and the Yorkshire Terriers.

Non Sporting Dogs

Boston Terrier

This group is made up of a miscellaneous collection of breeds with a wide variety of characteristics, sizes and backgrounds. They may now be generally classified as companion dogs.

Boston Terriers come in three sizes—under 15 pounds, 15 pounds but under 20, and 20 pounds but not over 25. They are brindle and white and usually have clipped ears, though in most of those not cropped the ears stand erect.

Bostons are short-headed. The muzzle is about one third the length of the skull and is shorter than its width and depth. The body is compact and the tail usually has a "screw" in it. The Boston continues to be one of the most popular breeds in shows and as pets.

Bulldog

Bulldogs, originally a fierce fighting dog developed for the specific purpose of bull-baiting, is now a peaceful and lovable companion. They are one of the world's most popular and best known breeds. Males average 50 pounds in weight and females 10 pounds less.

The under jaw is bent upward, and it is ideal when the teeth do not show when the mouth is closed. The head is massive and so is the body, with most of the weight being up front. The chest is very wide, with the body "swinging" between the legs. The top line dips behind the withers, then rises in a curve to the hips and falls away to the tail. The tail should not be carried above its root. Colors are red brindle, other brindles, solid white, solid red, fawn or piebald.

Dalmatian

The Dalmatian is the spotted dog once known as the "coach dog." He ranges from 19 to 23 inches at the shoulder and between 35 and 50 pounds. The spots should not run together. They should range from the size of a dime to a half dollar.

Dalmatians conform fairly well to sporting dogs in soundness but are not strongly angulated behind. The eyes can be dark in black-spotted dogs, yellow in liver-spotted. Wall or china eyes are permitted.

There are three varieties of Poodles. The Standard Poodle is 15 inches or more at the shoulder; the Miniature, under 15 but over 10; the Toy, 10 inches or under.

Poodle

Poodles can be shown until a year old in puppy clip (only the face and feet shaved). After that either the Continental or English Saddle Clip must be used. In the former, the hind quarters are shaved but pom-poms are left on the hips in some cases. The hind quarters are left covered with a blanket of hair in the English Saddle Clip.

Poodles come in solid colors only—white, black, chocolate, apricot, and silver. They conform to sporting dogs in soundness.

Dog Breeds and Registration

As America has grown, so has its dog population. Surveys show that, today, more than one out of every three families owns a dog. And many families own more than one dog.

Conservative estimates of the dog population place it at 37 million. We cannot estimate how many of these are purebred. No census based on this point has been attempted. Nor will stud book registration figures give us an idea. The reason is that more than half the dogs eligible for registration never are registered.

But the people who have tried to make area dog censuses are convinced that the purebreds gradually are creeping up on the mixed breeds. So that today, a fair guess is that there are 50 purebreds for every 50 mixed breeds. In former times as few as five per cent of the dogs were purebred.

One reason for the increase in purebreds is that livestock breeders the world over are becoming breed-conscious. And this interest in purebreds has carried over into dogs.

The American Kennel Club is currently registering nearly a million dogs annually. Other registration bodies register about 50,000 a year.

If you have a dog that is eligible for registration, you should have it registered.

If you are buying a purebred dog, be sure to get the papers for it, then have it registered immediately. You'll be thankful later. The breeder will give you an application to register the puppy, or a certificate of registration.

With most registration bodies, a dog cannot be registered unless its sire and dam have been registered, and unless the litter in which it was born also has been registered. Thus, the breeder usually gives the buyer an "application to register a puppy from a registered litter." You then fill in the name you are giving the dog, sign the form, and mail it in.

If the puppy is registered, you will get a registration certificate. You then have the dog transferred to your ownership. This is important, for unless you do, the dog may always be listed as belonging to someone else.

Popularity Of Various Breeds

Dog breeds vary in popularity as the years go by. But the shift is gradual and changes among the more popular breeds occur only every five to ten years. The American Kennel Club, the largest of the registration agencies, reports the breeds in the box below to be the most popular over recent years.

Poodles	Collies
German Shepherd Dogs	Pekingese
Irish Setters	Chihuahuas
Beagles	Shetland Sheepdogs
Dachshunds	Great Danes
Miniature Schnauzers	Brittany Spaniels
St. Bernards	Yorkshire Terriers
Doberman Pinschers	Golden Retrievers
Labrador Retrievers	Siberian Huskies
Cocker Spaniels	Lhasa Apsos

Registration Tips

At the time of purchase, *to insure registration* of your pup, the seller must give you one of three forms. (1) A blue A.K.C. application form to register an individual dog from a registered litter, or (2) A properly endorsed individual registration certificate transferring ownership to you, or (3) A signed bill of sale giving all the information listed in part 3 *below* if papers are not available at the moment. Do not accept a promise of later identification of the dog.

Examine the registration application forms you receive, and read the instructions and certifications on them. Make sure they are *complete and accurate* and that a separate certification has been completed and signed by each person through whose hands the dog has passed. Don't accept an application that appears to have been signed "in blank" (with only seller's signature) or that shows changes or erasures, unless each change has been initialed by the person who was required to complete that part of the form.

1. File application promptly with A.K.C. to register your dog, or to record transfer to your ownership if dog is already registered. You must record your ownership with AKC if the dog is to be bred or entered in AKC events.

2. Thousands of litters are advertised as "A.K.C. registered" although they are not, and possibly cannot be. Often this is because owners believe that an application to register a dog constitutes actual registration, or that a pedigree certificate is a certificate of registration and ownership. Before you buy, you are entitled to "see the proof."

3. Do not accept a word of mouth assurance that "the papers will come later." Demand a signed bill of sale which will provide full identification of the dog plus some assurance of an adjustment if for some reason your puppy cannot be registered with the American Kennel Club. A bill of sale for a puppy not yet registered must give the breed, sex, color and markings, date of birth, names and registration numbers of sire and dam, name of breeder, and litter registration number if the litter has already been registered. A bill of sale for a registered dog need list only the breed, registered name of the dog, and registration number. Both should include a provision for refund of part of purchase price if it develops that the seller cannot supply proper papers.

4. Never send cash with an application for registration. Money may be stolen from the mail. Your check or money order will prevent this and may make it possible to trace an application that is lost.

5. When you receive your official registration certificate, have it photostated. Keep the photostat in a separate file. If the original is lost, this will make it easier to get a duplicate.

6. Before using your own dog for breeding ask The American Kennel Club to send the proper forms for registering the litter and instructions for keeping the required records.

How to Understand a Dog Show

A dog show is, in one sense, a beauty contest of canines. Each breed has certain physical characteristics that make it different from other breeds. Each breed has an ideal for type and soundness. So a dog show is designed to prove the quality, or lack of it, of each dog.

In another sense, a dog show is an elimination contest, much as a tennis tournament would be. A show may start with 2,500 dogs and gradually eliminate them until a single dog is selected as the best-in-show winner.

There are regular classes for each breed: Puppy, Novice, American-bred, Bred-by-Exhibitor, and Open.

The Puppy class may be divided into classes for those six months but under nine, and those nine months but under 12. A dog over a year old on the day of the show cannot be shown in a puppy class.

The Novice class is for dogs over 6 months old that have not won a first prize in any class other than Puppy. After 3 first place wins in the Novice class a dog must be entered in Bred-by-Exhibitor, American-bred or the Open class.

The Bred-by-Exhibitor class is for A.K.C. registered dogs, except champions, owned by the breeder and shown by him or a member of his family.

The American bred class is for all dogs, except champions, born in the United States by reason of a mating that took place in this country.

The Open class is for all dogs. Champions may be entered, but seldom are. This is the only class in which foreign-bred dogs can compete, except that Canadian-bred puppies can compete in the Puppy class.

The winner of each of these classes gets a blue ribbon; second, a red one; third, a yellow, and fourth, a white.

There then is a winners' class. Each winner of a blue ribbon competes in this, unless he has been beaten in some other class. Since all of the classes, except in rare occasions, are divided by sex, there are two winners' classes. The winners of these get a purple ribbon while the second, or reserve winners, get a purple and white. The two winners are called "winners' dog" and "winners' bitch." They compete for best of winners, with the winner getting a blue and white ribbon.

Best Of Breed

It often happens that there will be champions entered who are competing for best of breed or higher honors. They now enter the ring and compete with the best of winners for best of breed. Best of breed is awarded a purple and gold ribbon. The best of opposite sex to the dog awarded "best of breed" is given a red and white ribbon.

Sometimes no best of breed is given. This is when a breed is divided into varieties as in Cocker Spaniels, Beagles, Dachshunds, and Poodles. Then a best-of-variety ribbon is awarded instead.

You will remember that all breeds recognized by the American Kennel Club are classified into groups, such as Sporting, Hound, etc. When all of the best-of-breed and best-of-variety winners in each group have been selected, these are brought back into the ring to compete for best in the group in which they belong.

Best In Show

The six group winners then compete for best in show. In that way, a show which might have started with 2,500 dogs ends up with one final grand victor.

There are a number of types of dog shows. Match or sanctioned shows operate under American Kennel Club sanction, but no championship points are allowed. Championship shows are called "licensed shows" since they operate under a license from the American Kennel Club. Another type of show is the "specialty." It is for one breed only, and can be sanctioned or licensed.

Championship points are awarded on a complicated bit of mathematics. This is worked out for various areas of the country, depending upon the general popularity of the breed, the numbers usually shown, and the popularity of the breed in that area. Only dogs getting purple *winners'* ribbons are eligible for championship points.

Dog show catalogs are required to carry the schedule of championship points for the area in which a given show is held. The following will give you an idea of how this works.

In the East and North division, a Dachshund of the smooth variety would get a championship point if three of his sex competed. He would get two points if six competed; three, if 11 competed; four, if there were 18; and five, if there were 31. The schedule for females often differs from that for males.

Dachshunds are very popular, both in numbers and in numbers shown. Among rarer breeds, six of one sex competing would mean five championship points for the winner. It is hardest for German Shepherds to win championships, since 62 males must compete to gain five points. For females, 64 must compete.

Although a dog must win 15 points to become a champion, he must win at least twice under different judges when there is a "three points or better" entry. Thus, a male German Shepherd competing in the New York area would have to defeat entries of 29 or more of its sex at least twice.

Obedience Trials

More than half the American dog shows now have obedience trials in conjunction with them. Obedience classes are Novice A and B, Open A and B, and Utility. Novice A and Open A are for people who are working their own dogs. If they have a second entry in the Novice division, it would have to be shown in Novice B. Professional trainers or a person handling someone else's dog can only enter in Novice B and Open B.

Utility is open to both professional and amateur trainers. A trainer can enter his dog in Open B and Utility, provided it has won its open title. The Novice title is Companion Dog, or CD. The Open title is Companion Dog Excellent, or CDX. The Utility title is Utility Dog (UD), or Utility Dog Tracking (UDT) if the dog has passed its tracking test also.

A dog cannot enter the Open classes until it has won its CD title. Nor can it enter the Utility class until it has won its CDX title. These titles are awarded by the American Kennel Club when the dog has earned the required number of points for each class.

If you were to see the name of a dog such as CH. Horsford Hetman UDT, you would know that Horsford Hetman had won his bench championship and the highest of all obedience-training awards as well. If Horsford Hetman was listed as Dual Ch., this would mean that he was both a bench and a field champion.

Show and Field Trial Wins

Event _____

Class _____ Placed _____

Event _____

Class _____ Placed _____

Event _____

Class _____ Placed _____

Training Your Dog for a Show

Two things are required of a dog at a dog show. He must trot on a leash without breaking stride, and he must stand quietly and in proper position for the judge to examine him. For these things he needs some training and some experience.

If you gave your dog obedience training, as outlined in an earlier chapter, then he already knows how to walk at your side. Now you must teach him to walk or trot while holding his head up. The reason for this is that the judge must check him for soundness of movement. If the dog's head is nosing along the ground, soundness of movement cannot be checked because the dog will be spreading his legs slightly as he moves and his head will block the judge's view.

Most people use a "show leash" at shows. This is a leash which serves as both collar and leash. You put the leash on the dog and tighten it so that it is firm about the throat but does not choke. The position of the collar part should be at the end of the neck so that, when the dog's head is raised, the leash is just back of the ears.

Moving along in this position you can give the dog light jerks to bring his head up. You can teach this in the house or along the sidewalk. Eventually you should practice in the presence of other dogs so that your pupil learns not to be distracted by them.

At dog shows it is required that the judge check gait when the dog is moving straight away from him and when he is coming directly toward him. Some handlers make a right or left turn at the end of the ring and thus give the judge a side view of the dog in motion. The judge may want this in breeds such as Dachshunds and Bassets, where there may be a tendency to sway-back when in motion. Always keep the dog between yourself and the judge.

The judge already will have seen all the dogs in motion together when they went around the ring so he may feel that the extra side view is merely wasting his time. This will be particularly true when the judge is behind schedule. It is a good idea to ask him: "Straight out and back?" Then he'll tell you what he wants.

Check dog books and magazines for pictures of champions of your breed. They will be posed as you will want to pose your dog in the show ring. At first your dog may refuse and you may have to slap him gently upward under the chin to remind him that he must obey you. First, he must hold his head up. Second, he must allow you to place his front legs in proper position. Third, he must let you place his hind legs and stand as you've posed him.

Take the front leg by one elbow, lift and place the foot so that the leg is perpendicular to the ground and solidly under him. Then take the other leg by the elbow and set it in the same way. Be sure that one foot is not ahead or behind the other and that the toes point straight ahead rather than out toward the side.

When you have taught him to stand while you do this you are ready to set his hind legs. The hind legs should be placed so that the back pasterns, often called the hocks, are perpendicular to the ground. Lean over the dog, take the stifle joint in your hand. lift one leg and place it. Then do the same with the other. The feet should be set far enough back so that stifle-joint angulation shows. Again, the hind feet should point straight ahead, turning neither in nor out. In general, the above instructions are correct for most breeds.

There are exceptions. With German Shepherds, one hind leg is brought forward and the tail is laid across the other, which

is drawn far back. Several breeds permit cow hocks (in which the hind feet point out at an angle rather than straight ahead). Chows are straight in stifles and you would not want to draw the hind legs back.

When you are teaching your dog to pose he may slump in the middle. In that case, slap him upward in the belly while commanding him to "Pose." Others will arch or roach their backs. They should get over this with practice. Gentle stroking pressure will help to level the back to the correct topline.

Your dog must permit examination of his teeth. Usually judges examine the front teeth only in order to see that the jaws are neither overshot (top jaw extends or protrudes beyond the lower) or undershot (the lower jaw extends beyond the upper).

Either condition means that a "level" or scissors bite does not exist. However, with dogs such as German Shepherds and Doberman Pinschers, premolars may be missing and the judge must check for this, too.

In Canada, judges are not permitted to put their fingers in dogs' mouths. Some American judges ask the owners or handlers to show the teeth. You will be extending a courtesy to the judge if you show him your dog's teeth and you may be helping to prevent spreading of disease. If you do show the teeth, it is only necessary to lift the lips. Do this honestly. If the dog is missing some teeth, don't try to hide the fact.

It is required of all judges that they check each male dog to see that he has two normal testicles, normally descended into the scrotum. Sometimes dogs do not like this examination. So you must practice with yours so that, in the show ring, he won't try to jerk away or sit down.

Finally, you must practice posing the dog and having other people examine him. When you can pose him and have others examine him in the presence of other dogs, then you can be sure your dog will act properly in the show ring.

Summary

The show dog has to learn to trot on leash and to stand for examination. Special leashes called "show leads" usually are used. Show dogs should trot with their heads up so that the soundness of their front movement can be seen. Dogs are taught to pose when standing for examination. You should try to pose your dog in the position seen in pictures of famous winners. Pose him in front of a mirror to check your ability. Before going to a show, display your dog to strangers and have them examine him so he will get used to the procedure.

Opportunities in the World of Dogs

Dog breeding is a sport and a hobby for thousands of people. Many make all or part of their living from dogs. It is possible for boys and girls to make a successful career in dogs.

Most people become interested in dog activities in haphazard fashion. They get a purebred dog, then someone invites them to join a club. They begin breeding and showing or they start training and running their dogs in field trials. All of a sudden they are full-fledged doggists.

Many of these people see opportunities dogdom offers them and enter the sport professionally. Sometimes they have children who become interested in dogs, too, and many of them grow up to make a career in some branch of the sport.

With this in mind let us examine some of the opportunities available and present some statistics:

Each year there are approximately 3,500 championship dog shows in the United States. Over half that number are all-breed events. There are more than 900 obedience trials and more than 1,000 field trials. In all of these, dogs can win points toward bench or field championships, "legs" toward obedience degrees.

What this means is that there are approximately 700 counties in the United States that have dog shows and at least 600 that hold field trials. Putting it another way, few counties in the United States are out of reach of those who want to engage in some form of dog activity.

The figures given are for American Kennel Club activities only. The United Kennel Club gives a couple of dozen bench shows for certain breeds which it registers, such as Toy Fox Terriers and Coonhounds. There are between 400 and 500 Coonhound field trials a year.

Some 10,000 Greyhounds are bred and registered in their own stud book each year and a majority of them get into coursing meets or to the race tracks. Greyhound racing is a legal sport in many states.

Usually it is not possible to make a living breeding dogs but some people do in the case of Greyhounds. Such people must have choice stock and they must breed carefully and well, else the financial return will not be great enough to support them.

Professional Handlers

Now let us return to dog shows. Many dogs are shown by professional handlers. About 1,000 handlers are licensed by the American Kennel Club. A professional handler is one who may board and train a dog to show and then show it for the owner. For this he charges a fee agreed upon for that show. Professional handlers use station wagons or estate trucks and may take many dogs to a single show.

Some professional handlers are people who started as breeders and who turned out to have a knack of showing dogs to their best advantage. Others were boys and girls who competed in junior showmanship classes, apprenticed as kennel helpers, and then became full-time handlers.

This is one sport in which girls compete on an equal basis with boys. In fact, it probably is true that there are more girl junior handlers than boys.

Professional handlers often arrange to take "strings" of dogs on "circuits"—a half dozen or more shows held in towns and cities fairly close together so that the dogs and handlers move from one to another quite easily. For example, there is the Deep South Circuit, the Florida Circuit, the South Texas Circuit, etc.

Some professional handlers have full-time jobs and go only to weekend dog shows. These handlers simply accept their clients' dogs at the shows. They bathe, trim, and groom them, and then take them into the ring. Others own large kennels and board dogs for the general public as well. Some may board, breed, and rear dogs of some clients.

Boarding And Breeding

This brings up another opportunity—the boarding kennel. A modern boarding kennel may cost $10,000 to $50,000 but most boarding kennel operations don't start on that scale. Instead a small building becomes a kennel, runs gradually are added, and enlargements and improvements made.

Operating a boarding kennel is rather hard work. However, it usually makes an excellent return on the investment and provides a comfortable living for thousands of people. There are few places left in American today that do not have boarding kennels. America's travel habits have also increased the need for boarding kennels.

Today's need is for kennels that have separate rooms for cats and even areas for parakeets and canaries. Both boarding kennels and professional handlers require helpers, and present an opportunity for young people to get started on a career.

Breeding of dogs can be a rewarding experience when you have a profitable demand for the pups.

Judges

Some handlers, both women and men, retire after a time to become judges. Also, some exhibitors get a license to judge their own breed, prove their worth, and gradually increase the number of breeds they judge.

The professional all-breed judge charges from $100 up per day, plus all expenses. If he had complete freedom, as in the case of a retired person, he could judge as many as 40 shows in the United States yearly and another dozen in Canada.

Dog Show Superintendents

Professional dog show superintendents are not too numerous. Yet every one started as a dog breeder and exhibitor or as a handler. One present-day superintendent simply grew up in the game. As a boy of 14, he began to go to dog shows with his neighbor who was a superintendent. He helped out at the shows and at 21 became a full-time licensed superintendent. These people are the highest income earners in the dog game.

Most superintendents need help, and it is possible for boys and girls to get weekend jobs with them. Being a dog show superintendent may seem like a doubtful job for a woman but there are at least five in the United States.

Veterinarians

Many boys and girls decide to become veterinarians. After

completing high school, 3-4 years of college education are required prior to entering veterinary college (4 yrs. course). Competition is stiff and good grades are essential. The veterinary profession is a most satisfying way of life offering many opportunities for public services. Your veterinarian is the safeguard of animal health.

Field Trainers

Thus far, we have not spoken of field trials and just plain hunting dogs. Today field trials are growing rapidly in proportion as game diminishes. For the field trial is really hunting under controlled conditions. At a field trial you can almost be certain your dog will find game within a few minutes to an hour while on a hunt you might go all day without finding any.

Today, there is a greater need for field trainers than for skilled career people in any other branch of the dog game. People want their dogs trained for hunting because they realize that a trained, experienced dog is much more likely to find game.

They may want their dog trained to retrieve because they know the dog that can mark a fall, track a runner, and bring the crippled bird to the gamebag is one of great value. Such a dog makes his owner stay within the bag limit. The cripples do not escape to die while the hunter shoots other game.

Most field trainers became professionals after training their own dogs and after finding they have a knack for it. Others served as apprentices, or helpers, to established trainers. Here again, women can compete on an equal basis with men. Some of the finest field trial trainers in dogdom are women.

Field trainers make good incomes. They, too, travel about the country and have the finest people for their clients.

Dog Trainers

Still another training field is that of obedience. Hundreds of people make their living by training dogs in obedience. They may train dogs for obedience contests or they may just take problem dogs and cure their bad habits. Some may operate large classes in the summer to augment their income.

Some are former Army war dog trainers. Some learned their trade at guide-dog schools for the blind. Others trained their dogs for obedience contests, were conspicuously successful, and finally became professional trainers.

There is almost no limit to the possibilities for obedience training. Chief reason for this is the increasing number of dogs in cities and the increase in the stringency of city dog laws.

Since their beginning in 1934, obedience-training classes have sprung up everywhere. Many cities and towns have brought in trainers to organize classes in connection with school adult-recreation programs.

As with professional handlers and field trainers, many obedience trainers operate boarding kennels, too. If they have half an acre of ground behind the kennels they can organize summer training classes.

Such classes usually have 25 to 30 dogs and owners and last for 10 to 11 weeks. The owner is charged a fee for the course and is taught how to train his own dog. Classes are held once a week. School gymnasiums often are used in the winters, as are armories or parking garages.

Dog Writers

There are perhaps 75 newspapers that employ dog writers. Sometimes these are reporters who have made dogs a specialty and have added a dog column and news reports of shows and trials. Some have made dogs and pets such an important part of the paper that they write on nothing else. A few are not newspaper people but simply write a weekly column on dog activities. This field is unlimited. Any boy or girl who begins as an apprentice newspaperman and who already is skilled in dogs will find a place for his column.

Writers on dogs also sometimes become editors and owners

of magazines. They sell articles to general magazines and they write books on dogs. Dog books often pay very well. If directed toward a particular market—that is, a particular breed—a good sale is assured. Dog books almost always earn more money than do the majority of novels.

Radio and television programs also are a possibility for the boy or girl who decides to make dogs a career. Dog photographers are highly paid and in much demand.

The Dog Industry

Finally, there are increasing opportunities in the pet industry. Many millions of dollars are spent every year for dog foods, dog equipment, and dog medicine. This is big business—offering good-paying jobs for salesmen; for persons skilled in production, research, and advertising; and for managers and other executives.

Those of you who wish to combine your enjoyment of dogs with a business career might consider this advice: Learn everything you can about dogs *and* their owners. Get experience by working in a pet store or any place where dog foods or supplies are made or sold. Complete your education and try to determine your special interest, whether it is selling, production or research. Then apply for a job with the knowledge that the dog industry needs and will hire young people who have knowledge and ideas about what appeals to dogs—and their owners.

Summary

Boys and girls who want a career in the world of dogs can start as kennel helpers, as aids to professional handlers or field trainers, or as junior showmanship handlers showing their own or other people's dogs. Dog enthusiasts can establish pet shops, become dog photographers, become field or obedience trainers, or train problem dogs. They can become dog writers, dog show superintendents, veterinarians, or enter any one of a number of careers connected with the production and sale of dog food and equipment.

References:
Dollars In Dogs,
by Leon F. Whitney, DVM.
Practical Science

STORE COUPON

TO THE CONSUMER: Caution! Please don't embarrass your Retailer by asking him to redeem coupons without making the required purchase. He must redeem coupons properly to get his money back. Remember, coupons are good only on the brands called for. Any other use constitutes fraud. Please don't redeem coupons that have expired.

RETAILER: For payment of face value, plus 7¢ handling, send to Ralston Purina Company, P.O. Box PL1, Belleville, Illinois 62222. Coupon will be paid only if presented by a retailer of our merchandise or a clearing house approved by us and acting for and at the risk of the retailer. Retailer must submit on request invoices proving purchases of sufficient stock within normal redemption cycle to cover the merchandising program represented by coupons presented for redemption. This coupon is nontransferable, nonassignable, nonreproducible and any sales tax must be paid by customer. Offer good only in U.S.A., A.P.O.'s, F.P.O.'s and void where prohibited, taxed, or otherwise restricted. Cash redemption value 1/20 of 1¢.

LIMIT ONE COUPON PER PURCHASE OF ANY SIZE OR FLAVOR PURINA DOG CHOW DOG FOOD. ANY USE NOT CONSISTENT WITH THESE TERMS CONSTITUTES FRAUD AND MAY VOID ALL COUPONS SUBMITTED FOR REDEMPTION.

DOG CARE HANDBOOK

25¢   290 ◁DC▷ 290   **25¢**

STORE COUPON

TO THE CONSUMER: Caution! Please don't embarrass your Retailer by asking him to redeem coupons without making the required purchase. He must redeem coupons properly to get his money back. Remember, coupons are good only on the brands called for. Any other use constitutes fraud. Please don't redeem coupons that have expired.

RETAILER: For payment of face value, plus 7¢ handling, send to Ralston Purina Company, P.O. Box PL1, Belleville, Illinois 62222. Coupon will be paid only if presented by a retailer of our merchandise or a clearing house approved by us and acting for and at the risk of the retailer. Retailer must submit on request invoices proving purchases of sufficient stock within normal redemption cycle to cover the merchandising program represented by coupons presented for redemption. This coupon is nontransferable, nonassignable, nonreproducible and any sales tax must be paid by customer. Offer good only in U.S.A., A.P.O.'s, F.P.O.'s and void where prohibited, taxed, or otherwise restricted. Cash redemption value 1/20 of 1¢.

LIMIT ONE COUPON PER PURCHASE OF ANY SIZE OR FLAVOR PURINA PUPPY CHOW. ANY USE NOT CONSISTENT WITH THESE TERMS CONSTITUTES FRAUD AND MAY VOID ALL COUPONS SUBMITTED FOR REDEMPTION.

DOG CARE HANDBOOK

  173 PC 173

STORE COUPON

TO THE CONSUMER: Caution! Please don't embarrass your Retailer by asking him to redeem coupons without making the required purchase. He must redeem coupons properly to get his money back. Remember, coupons are good only on the brands called for. Any other use constitutes fraud. Please don't redeem coupons that have expired.

RETAILER: For payment of face value, plus 7¢ handling, send to Ralston Purina Company, P.O. Box PL1, Belleville, Illinois 62222. Coupon will be paid only if presented by a retailer of our merchandise or a clearing house approved by us and acting for and at the risk of the retailer. Retailer must submit on request invoices proving purchases of sufficient stock within normal redemption cycle to cover the merchandising program represented by coupons presented for redemption. This coupon is nontransferable, nonassignable, nonreproducible and any sales tax must be paid by customer. Offer good only in U.S.A., A.P.O.'s, F.P.O.'s and void where prohibited, taxed, or otherwise restricted. Cash redemption value 1/20 of 1¢.

LIMIT ONE COUPON PER PURCHASE OF ANY SIZE OF PURINA HIGH PROTEIN DOG MEAL. ANY USE NOT CONSISTENT WITH THESE TERMS CONSTITUTES FRAUD AND MAY VOID ALL COUPONS SUBMITTED FOR REDEMPTION.

DOG CARE HANDBOOK

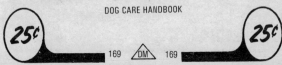

169 DM 169

STORE COUPON

TO THE CONSUMER: Caution! Please don't embarrass your Retailer by asking him to redeem coupons without making the required purchase. He must redeem coupons properly to get his money back. Remember, coupons are good only on the brands called for. Any other use constitutes fraud. Please don't redeem coupons that have expired.

RETAILER: For payment of face value, plus 7¢ handling, send to Ralston Purina Company, P.O. Box PL1, Belleville, Illinois 62222. Coupon will be paid only if presented by a retailer of our merchandise or a clearing house approved by us and acting for and at the risk of the retailer. Retailer must submit on request invoices proving purchases of sufficient stock within normal redemption cycle to cover the merchandising program represented by coupons presented for redemption. This coupon is nontransferable, nonassignable, nonreproducible and any sales tax must be paid by customer. Offer good only in U.S.A., A.P.O.'s, F.P.O.'s and void where prohibited, taxed, or otherwise restricted. Cash redemption value 1/20 of 1¢.

LIMIT ONE COUPON PER PURCHASE OF ANY SIZE OR FLAVOR PURINA CHUCK WAGON DOG FOOD. ANY USE NOT CONSISTENT WITH THESE TERMS CONSTITUTES FRAUD AND MAY VOID ALL COUPONS SUBMITTED FOR REDEMPTION.

DOG CARE HANDBOOK

30¢ ———— 322 △CW 322 ———— 30¢

STORE COUPON

TO THE CONSUMER: Caution! Please don't embarrass your Retailer by asking him to redeem coupons without making the required purchase. He must redeem coupons properly to get his money back. Remember, coupons are good only on the brands called for. Any other use constitutes fraud. Please don't redeem coupons that have expired.

RETAILER: For payment of face value, plus 7¢ handling, send to Ralston Purina Company, P.O. Box PL1, Belleville, Illinois 62222. Coupon will be paid only if presented by a retailer of our merchandise or a clearing house approved by us and acting for and at the risk of the retailer. Retailer must submit on request invoices proving purchases of sufficient stock within normal redemption cycle to cover the merchandising program represented by coupons presented for redemption. This coupon is nontransferable, nonassignable, nonreproducible and any sales tax must be paid by customer. Offer good only in U.S.A., A.P.O.'s, F.P.O.'s and void where prohibited, taxed, or otherwise restricted. Cash redemption value 1/20 of 1¢.

LIMIT ONE COUPON PER PURCHASE OF PURINA FIT & TRIM DOG FOOD. ANY USE NOT CONSISTENT WITH THESE TERMS CONSTITUTES FRAUD AND MAY VOID ALL COUPONS SUBMITTED FOR REDEMPTION.

DOG CARE HANDBOOK

25¢   70 △FT 70   25¢

25¢   STORE COUPON   25¢

TO THE CONSUMER: Caution! Please don't embarrass your Retailer by asking him to redeem coupons without making the required purchase. He must redeem coupons properly to get his money back. Remember, coupons are good only on the brands called for. Any other use constitutes fraud. Please don't redeem coupons that have expired.

RETAILER: For payment of face value, plus 7¢ handling, send to Ralston Purina Company, P.O. Box PL1, Belleville, Illinois 62222. Coupon will be paid only if presented by a retailer of our merchandise or a clearing house approved by us and acting for and at the risk of the retailer. Retailer must submit on request invoices proving purchases of sufficient stock within normal redemption cycle to cover the merchandising program represented by coupons presented for redemption. This coupon is nontransferable, nonassignable, nonreproducible and any sales tax must be paid by customer. Offer good only in U.S.A., A.P.O.'s, F.P.O.'s and void where prohibited, taxed, or otherwise restricted. Cash redemption value 1/20 of 1¢.

LIMIT ONE COUPON PER PURCHASE OF ANY SIZE PURINA DOG CHOW MOIST & CHUNKY DOG FOOD. ANY USE NOT CONSISTENT WITH THESE TERMS CONSTITUTES FRAUD AND MAY VOID ALL COUPONS SUBMITTED FOR REDEMPTION.

DOG CARE HANDBOOK

25¢   54 △MC 54   25¢